The
Lake to Lake
Walk

The
Lake to Lake
Walk

Alistair Wallace

M C Publications

First published in 1999 by
M C Publications
The Memoir Club
The Old School
New Road
Crook Town
Durham

British Library Cataloguing in
Publication Data.
A catalogue record for this book
is available from the
British Library.

ISBN: 1 84104-006-1

Printed by Lintons Printers, Crook, County Durham.

To my wife Jackie

Acknowledgements

I would like to thank the following individuals and companies for the support they have shown throughout the production of this book:

Jackie, Heather & Kevin, Dave Clough, Sue Reay, Chris Lines, Berghaus Ltd., Terra Nova Equipment Ltd., Peri Langdale, Tyne Tees Television, The Camera Crews from Tyne Tees, Sir Chris Bonington, Martin Fenwick, Elaine Mills, Paul, Villa Soft Drinks Ltd., Rab Carrington Ltd., Steve & Angie Trippitt, Durham County Libraries Tourist Information Centres, David Tarn, Peter & Linda Stenson, Glynn & Ann Brown, Dennis & Mary Walker, Sykeside Camping Park, Riverside Leisure, The Durham Dales Centre, John Wallace, Linda & Roger Furlong, Ray Allinson, Paul Reach, *Country Walking Magazine*, Jeff Watson, Jimmy Lawrence, The Camera Clinic, Simon Goodwin, Linda Hutchinson and The Durham Youth Enterprise Scheme.

My thanks also go to the people who live along the corridor of this route. Their hospitality and friendship is something I will remember for life.

Book cover photograph by David Tarn

Contents

Foreword by Sir Christian Bonington CBE

People often ask me, especially on my return from a Himalayan expedition, if I find the British hills an anticlimax after the giant peaks of Nepal and Tibet. Nothing could be further from the truth. Towards the end of a long expedition I am always homesick for our beautiful northern hills and the Lake District Fells in particular. I never tire of the gentle rolling slopes of High Pike which sweep up behind our cottage, and Wendy, my wife, and I like nothing better than to walk there with our dogs. The light is never the same twice, varying with the weather and the seasons or even the time of day.

Although I haven't completed *The Lake to Lake* route, I have walked in most of the areas through which it passes, and it seems to me that it must be one of the most beautiful and varied of the long distance trails. Starting in southern Lakeland with its tree clad valleys and craggy fells, it winds its way through the more barren, rock-strewn slopes of Scandale to Patterdale and the shores of Ullswater. Leaving the hills behind it meanders along the gentle Eden Valley before climbing once more into the windswept heights of the Pennines and the desolate, largely abandoned mining areas of Teesdale and Weardale.

Historic Hexham is a welcome contrast before crossing the Roman Wall and heading north via Bellingham and Falstone to journey's end at Keilder Water.

Walking is a pastime which can be enjoyed by all, whether just for a modest few miles a day or on a multi-mile, long distance trek. It is a way of quietly using the countryside which brings benefits far beyond those of just recreation. It offers the chance to refresh lives that are increasingly stressed, and ruled by technology. Many more people are using the footpaths and participating in the long distance walks, so with increased use must come increased responsibility. We must all develop an awareness of the impact being made on the environment, try to keep it to a minimum and, as far as possible, leave no trace of our passing.

It would be nice to think of future generations enjoying *The Lake To Lake Walk* and finding there the same unspoilt beauty as exists today.

Introduction

A shimmering haze hovers over the valley below where thatched cottage chimney stacks gently bellow wisps of smoke and an oak beamed Inn stands with hearty fire and lashings of food all cooked on an open range by a cheery landlord.

Muscles scream out for relief, limbs ache in places you didn't realise existed, the rain and sleet is whisked up the valley by high winds and bite into your face like stinging pine needles and you still have the prospect of yet another gut wrenching climb before reaching your overnight goal.

Two descriptions of England's green and pleasant land. Should you wish to comfort yourself and believe the first statement then long distance walks are not what you are looking for. However, if you can empathise with the second statement then read on because, as a hiker, you are about to discover the birth of a new walk, a walk that will take you over some of the most rugged and spectacular terrain and through the very heart of this beautiful country.

Over many years, more than I care to admit, I have tackled most of the excellent long distance walks laid down by others and always dreamed of one day formulating my own route. I studied many writers during this time but there was one who really made me think, a man who always said, 'Don't follow my routes, go out and create your own', a man who was without equal in this field. He was, of course, Alf Wainwright.

After walking the great man's *Coast to Coast* and looking in depth at the work that must have gone into its design I spent many lonely hours contemplating the thought of producing something on the same scale. Unfortunately I was committed to writing other books and therefore my dream would have to be put on hold for a number of years.

In 1996 everything suddenly changed, I was approached by Durham County Council and asked to resurrect a long distance trail through the county which had fallen into oblivion. As I researched this ancient walk I was amazed at the history which I unearthed in the region.

By the time The Weardale Way was launched in 1997 (and is now a very popular walk) I started to realise that maybe, just maybe, my dream was within reach.

There were some very lucrative offers on the table from various forms of media and to be honest I was tempted. However, with the backing of my long suffering wife and my sponsors at Berghaus I decided that now was the time to go for that dream and so the initial seeds of *The Lake to Lake* were sown.

Two years, countless hours of research and after more than eight hundred miles of walking, I finally settled on a route which encompassed everything our sport is about.

Superb scenery, invigorating walking, historical interest and good overnight facilities all combine to make the walk that you are about to witness one to remember.

As someone who always backpacks I am well aware of the lack of information given on this subject and therefore have tried to redress the balance and provide a full guide for such hardy souls.

The walk starts in Bowness on the shores of Lake Windermere and does so as a tribute to The Dales Way which finishes here and was the subject of my very first book. The actual starting point is at the Royal Oak where a register is held for those venturing out.

The route takes us north through the Lakes and along the shores of Ullswater before veering eastwards across the country. As once again the walk turns northwards we venture into an area which has always been largely and somewhat unfairly forgotten by hikers, the North Pennines.

The dales of Teesdale, Weardale and Allendale all provide rugged terrain and battle scarred history whilst at the same time offering the kind of hospitality that only this region can.

The three great rivers, Tees, Wear and Tyne, are all crossed in their infancy stages before the walk finally arrives at its destination on the tree lined banks of Kielder.

The Lake to Lake which meanders its way from the largest lake in England gently up country to the largest man-made lake was one man's dream and I hope you enjoy sharing in that dream. As for me, I am off to research a new coastline walk. Where? Well, you will have to wait for the next book to find out.

Preparations for the Walk

The *Lake To Lake* is not presently waymarked and therefore provides a stern challenge to all who undertake this walk.

The following section is designed for the less experienced hiker and deals with aspects such as safety, equipment and planning.

Through many years of experience I have witnessed on numerous occasions walkers putting themselves and others into dangerous and unfortunately sometimes fatal situations, simply because they were not prepared for the task they were undertaking. Hiking is basically a safe sport but only when stringent guidelines are followed.

The hiker who follows the rules, takes all possible precautions and is prepared for any eventuality will invariably have a safe and highly enjoyable trek.

The walk you are about to undertake crosses some of the most hostile terrain this country has to offer. The Lake District and the North Pennines can catch out even the most experienced hiker and therefore you must be prepared. It is always better to carry those extra few pounds of weight if it enhances your chances of a safe return.

Many years ago as I trained for the Duke of Edinburgh's Gold Award I was given a piece of advice which has stood me in good stead ever since, **E...S...P**

EQUIPMENT........SAFETY........PLANNING

and by remembering ESP the foundations for a long and safe venture into fellwalking are well and truly laid, whether it be a low level Dales walk or a more adventurous trek into the mountains.

EQUIPMENT

The range of equipment carried is of course a personal choice and will vary depending on whether you are backpacking or not but there are certain items which are essential to all categories of walkers. Some of these items may never be put to the test but if carried could and would save your life.

In recent years the Outdoor Pursuits Industry has made huge strides in the production of top quality lightweight equipment. Admittedly, some of this equipment is very expensive but will last a lifetime and, at the end of the day, what is more important, your bank balance or your life?

For many years I have worn Berghaus equipment (even before I was sponsored by them) and found it unbeatable when in a difficult spot. So what equipment is needed before venturing out into the hills? Before each and every expedition I have a stringent check list which I meticulously adhere to. Only designed as a guide this is the equipment I carry.

Sturdy Walking Boots - the range of boots today can vary from £20 to £200, with the quality varying accordingly. Having warm and dry feet will make the walk so much more enjoyable. Personal choice - Storm Goretex boots from Berghaus.

Walking Socks - sports socks tend to be ideal as an under sock whilst 100% wool socks will be of huge benefit as an outer. Try to avoid nylon as this will tend to make the feet hot and therefore prone to blistering.

Walking Trousers - these should be light and allow unrestricted movement. Avoid denim at all costs. When wet jeans become heavy and will sap energy quickly. They also take an age to dry out. Personal Choice - Powerstretch Polartec Pants.

Underwear - they may not be everyone's idea of 'haute couture' but the old fashioned long johns are still in a class of their own.

Shirt - try to wear something light. Once on the move body heat will rise quite quickly and if too warm will start to sap energy. Personal Choice - Polartec lightweight top.

Fleece or other outer garment - whilst walking the body heat is maintained but diminishes quickly when stationary. It is therefore essential to have something to slip on quickly during short breaks. Personal Choice - Windbloc Polartec Fleece.

Waterproofs - an essential part of any hiker's equipment, the need for good quality waterproofs cannot be stressed too highly as these will make the difference between a walk being highly enjoyable and totally miserable. There is nothing more uncomfortable or more dangerous than being soaked through to the skin. An investment in top quality gear will reap rewards. Personal Choice - Summer months - Berghaus Helium Goretex Coat, Winter - Berghaus Manislu Goretex Shell. Trousers - Berghaus Goretex Leggings. Expensive but worth every penny.

Gaiters - whilst the rain may have ceased the terrain can often be wet and gaiters will provide protection from the knees downwards against the elements.

Hat and Gloves - more than 70% of all body heat is lost through the head and it is therefore vital to carry a hat at all times. Likewise gloves, keep all extremities warm. Personal Choice - Polartec Spire Hat and Windbloc gloves. I also carry Goretex mitts for adverse weather conditions.

Spare Clothing - always carry spare clothing. It is a lovely feeling at the end of a day if you can have a shower and change your clothes. Try not to fall into the trap of carrying too much in the way of spares. It is only extra weight to be lugged around on your back. Personal Choice - one pair of lightweight trousers, Polartec top and jumper.

OTHER ESSENTIAL ITEMS

Maps of the area - Ordnance Survey maps of the area you are walking are essential, as is the ability to read those maps. If you are in any doubt as to your ability a visit to your local library should be able to reveal where tuition can be found.

Compass - again essential. Knowing how to use a compass can literally save your life and a good knowledge of its working provides you and everyone with you with a sense of security.

Guide Book - essential to the author that you each buy one. I have a living to make. Seriously, the guide book is only there as a point of reference and so your own skills of route detection should be trusted.

First Aid Kit - a comprehensive kit should always be carried. You never know when it will be needed, either for someone in your own party or for someone you should come across on the course of your venture. If walking in a large party a minimum of two kits should be carried. Survival Bag - to work in conjunction with the first aid kit.

Whistle and Torch - more safety items that are essential.

Emergency Ration Pack - ideally enough food for a 24 hour period. Ideal items to include are the likes of Mars Bars, Nuts and Raisins and Kendal Mint Cake.

Sundries - toiletries, towel, pen and pencil, spare boot laces, spare batteries and spare whistle.

Rucksack - when selecting a rucksack from the vast array currently available on the market always ensure you choose one which will suit your needs. There is little point in purchasing a 25 litre (rucksack sizes are normally quoted in litre capacity) sack if you are intending a multi day walk. A good guide to follow is that if you are doing a walk staying at B&Bs etc. then you will need a sack of not less than 45 litre capacity. Should you be backpacking then you are looking in the range of 70 litres. Today most rucksacks are water resistant. However, it is still a good tip to wrap everything in plastic bags before loading them into the sack. Better safe than sorry.

BACKPACK OR B&B ?

Today the vast majority of hikers choose to stay at B&Bs along the route. The prospect of a warm bath and bed for the night is sorely tempting and you are not burdened with the extra weight and as you relax in a bath the backpacker has to set up camp for the night.

Backpacking however does have some distinct advantages over its B&B counterpart. You have the freedom to stop whenever you like, the cost is minimal and you are not governed by breakfast as to when you want to start walking. It has to be said that most of the people backpacking are in their younger years (with the exception of one cranky old author) and prefer to save their hard earned cash for an evening in some local hostelry. Should you decide to backpack you will be carrying far in excess of the normal 'load' which is very demanding. A good level of fitness is vital for a backpacking adventure.

EXTRA EQUIPMENT REQUIRED BY BACKPACKERS

Tent - with the exception of waterproofs your tent selection is the most crucial. It needs to be totally waterproof yet light in weight.

Whenever you select a tent try it out first. I tend to erect it in my garden and turn the hosepipe on it, that way I find out in advance its capabilities. Once again you only get what you pay for but remember that this will be your home for a couple of weeks. Personal Choice - I always use the Solar from Terra Nova Equipment Ltd., which is a totally waterproof one man tent and yet weighs less than 2kg.

Sleeping Bag - keeping warm is crucial and therefore so is the selection of bag. However it needs to be lightweight and compact when folded. Personal Choice - whenever I am planning an expedition I always contact Rab Carrington Ltd. in Sheffield. This company can put you onto the exact sleeping bag you require for your venture and the prices are exceptionally reasonable.

Stove and Gas - once again lightweight is the key word. Personal Choice - I use an Alpine stove using Colman gas canisters available at all good camping shops. I do tend to keep well away from Camping Gaz. The stoves are good but the canisters have a very short life span.

Food - the choice of food carried is a personal one but it is best to stay clear of tinned foods (weight). Good camping shops now provide a reasonable selection of freeze dried foods which are quite acceptable. Tea, coffee and sugar etc. all need to be carried.

Tip - I usually use the likes of Pot Noodles and similar pasta dishes. Once removed from their packaging they can be put into plastic bags and stored very easily.

Other basic requirements - bedroll, billies, plate, cup, bowl, cutlery, can opener, toilet roll.

SAFETY ON THE FELLS

Having the right equipment is only the first stage towards ensuring not only your safety but the safety of others you may meet on the walk. Hiking is predominantly a safe sport but accidents will inevitably occur. The only alarming fact about hiking is that when an accident does occur it will, more than likely, be miles away from the nearest point of help. Therefore it is imperative for the hiker to take every possible precaution to minimise those risks and be ready to deal with them when they do happen.

Walking alone creates the greatest risk and, whilst many walkers prefer to walk alone, yours truly amongst them, it is far safer to walk as a part of an organised group.

By learning basic techniques in First Aid, map reading and compass work confidence is achieved in handling any situation. When a map or book refers to a 'footpath' it often means a barely visible trampling of earth regularly crossing tree roots and loose boulders. A sprain or worse is always a distinct possibility and you must be able to deal with it.

A few classes during the long winter months will reap huge benefits when out on the hills. Your local library will put you in touch with places where you can get instruction on the likes of First Aid and Map Reading.

Prior to any walk the route for the day should be planned and logged with a responsible adult, giving as much information as possible, including your expected time of arrival at your destination. Leaving the route with the proprietor of your previous evening's accommodation is a good way of the authorities being informed in case of mishap. When arriving at your destination it is imperative you contact that person and inform them of your safe arrival otherwise the valuable time of the rescue services will be needlessly wasted.

Once decided and logged it is in your own interests to stick to the route. If something untoward should happen it will save precious time if the rescue teams know where to start looking.

ACCIDENTS

Understandably, when an accident occurs panic sets in very quickly but being able to remain calm and assess the situation will benefit everyone, especially the casualty.

Check the injured person and try to determine the extent of their injuries. It may be that with a sprain or something similar you may be able to get them to safety without the need of a rescue team. If you are in any doubt as to whether it would be safe to move the patient then leave them exactly where they are, administer first aid where appropriate and make sure they are warm by getting them into a survival bag (and tent if carried).

Do not go charging off for help at this point. Firstly take a triangulation to determine your exact whereabouts, make a note of the grid reference and hand it to the person(s) going for help, then check the map to see where the nearest point of help may be. Beware, as many buildings marked on OS maps can be derelict remains. Check especially for marked telephone boxes.

Once decided, leave a copy of the route with the person(s) remaining with the casualty (wherever possible at least one person should remain with the injured party to ensure they remain conscious). Do not give the patient any estimations of how long a rescue may take. If it takes longer than anticipated morale will sap and the situation becomes even more serious. Now is the time to set off for help armed with the grid reference point of the casualty's location. Of course the tendency is to run but if another accident occurs now then the scenario will be bleak so the best idea is to walk briskly instead .

On reaching the nearest point of help dial 999 and ask for 'Mountain Rescue'. You will then be connected to the nearest Police Station who will co-ordinate the rescue. Remembering to give the officer the grid reference point, listen carefully and follow their explicit instructions.

Now this is all very well if you are a member of a party but what if you are alone or with only one other person? If you are alone then your fate is in your own hands. If you are unable to continue or doubtful in any way then try to keep yourself warm first and foremost. Put on extra clothing and try to get into your survival bag, take the whistle and start sounding the distress signal. This is six blasts on the whistle every minute. If dark then emit the same signal with both torch and whistle. If you have logged your route as suggested it will only be a matter of time before you are located but be prepared, you may have a lengthy wait.

Should you be walking with one other person who gets injured then a decision has to be made as to whether or not it would be safe to leave the casualty and seek help. Follow the guidelines already mentioned but if you are in any doubt whatsoever stay exactly where you are and start giving the distress signals.

By now you have probably decided that this walking game is far too dangerous and a night in front of the 'telly' seems more appealing but be assured the sport of hiking is predominantly safe. With good training you will probably never get into this situation. This section is here just in case it did happen. In more than thirty years of mountaineering I have had just one minor injury.

PLANNING

Before attempting any long distance walk you must know your limitations. The experienced walker already knows how far they feel comfortable walking each day but for the novice it really is a trip into the unknown. Much will depend on the level of your fitness before deciding on a suitable format.

Weekend walks are without doubt the best way to find what distances suit you and also give the opportunity not only to test your abilities with map and compass but also to gain valuable experience in carrying extra weight on your back for more than just a day. A multi day walk is very different to a day jaunt. The limbs have a very short recovery time and the constant pounding of boot on earth is very draining.

After a couple of weekend hikes it should be possible to determine the distance you are comfortable walking each day. This is a personal choice and therefore the decision should be made by you and you alone. There is little point in over-estimating your capabilities. All that will happen is that you will have a thoroughly miserable time and never want to see another mountain again. You know your limitations; stick to them and don't let anyone else influence you.

Many years ago, as a young and sprightly fool I used to work on twenty miles a day. What a waste. I was so preoccupied with pounding out the miles I failed to comprehend the whole concept of walking. As soon as I slowed down and took notice of my environment I started learning about this new world, a world that could teach me so much.

Today when I plan a walk I aim to cover no more than ten to twelve miles. This gives me time to enjoy the countryside and villages that I pass through and at the same time have a relaxing pace that will not leave me a crumpled heap at the end of the day.

There are times however when extra miles must be covered and you must be prepared for this happening. When the route is planned there is every likelihood that at some stage there will not be a campsite or B&B within your range and so it may be neccesary to continue on for a few miles more.

When planning a multi-day walk the route should be broken down into comfortable sections taking into account the terrain. For example the section of this walk which goes over Scandale Pass in the Lakes means a climb of 2,000 feet therefore mileage that day is severely reduced. Facilities for planned breaks and accommodation for the following night all need to be considered carefully.

Where possible it is always advisable to book well in advance for accommodation. The areas this walk goes through, especially the Lake District, are very popular.

Mileage Charts

Whilst daily walking distances are very much an individual concern the following chart shows how I personally broke the walk down into comfortable sections. Twice during this epic walk I deliberately reduced mileage, at Appleby and at Chesters Roman Fort. This served a dual purpose, not only did I have time to discover the delights of the places mentioned but it also gave extra time for the limbs to recover.

To complete the Lake To Lake you will need the following landranger 1:50000 maps: 80, 87, 90, 91, 92, 97

DAY	FROM	DESTINATION	MILES	TOTAL
One	Royal Oak, Bowness	Ambleside Centre	9.0	9.0
14 Miles	Ambleside Centre	Sykeside	5.0	14.0
Two	Sykeside	Side Farm	3.4	17.4
14.9 Miles	Side Farm	Howtown	6.0	23.4
	Howtown	Pooley Bridge	5.5	28.9
Three	Pooley Bridge	Helton	3.7	32.6
10.7 Miles	Helton	Sheriff Park	3.0	35.6
	Sheriff Park	Newby Arms Hotel	4.0	39.6
Four	Newby Arms Hotel	Burwain Hall	4.0	43.6
7.7 Miles	Burwain Hall	Appleby	3.7	47.3
Five	Appleby	Little Ormside	3.2	50.5
10.1 Miles	Little Ormside	Ploughlands Farm	3.6	54.1
	Ploughlands Farm	Brough	4.3	57.4

DAY	FROM	DESTINATION	MILES	TOTAL
Six	Brough	Balderhead Reservoir	8.7	66.1
15.5 Miles	Balderhead Reservoir	Middleton in Teesdale	6.8	72.9
Seven	Middleton in Teesdale	Bollihope	7.5	80.4
12.2 Miles	Bollihope	Stanhope	4.7	85.1
Eight	Stanhope	Rookhope	8.0	93.1
14.5 Miles	Rookhope	The Allenheads Inn	6.5	99.6
Nine	The Allenheads Inn	Allendale	10.5	110.1
10.5 Miles				
Ten	Allendale	Dipton Mill	7.75	117.85
11.5 Miles	Dipton Mill	Hexham	3.75	121.6
Eleven	Hexham	Humshaugh	8.4	130.0
8.4 Miles				
Twelve	Humshaugh	High Moralee Farm	8.0	138.0
17.25 Miles	High Moralee Farm	Bellingham	9.25	147.25
Final Day	Bellingham	Cadger Ford	6.5	153.75
15.25 Miles	Cadger Ford	Kielder Reservoir	9.25	163.0

The mileages shown are for the direct routes and do not include any extra distance covered using the alternative routes.

ALTERNATIVE ROUTES

As the trek reaches the North Pennines I have included some alternative routes which should be seriously considered if you are not proficient in map and compass work.

IN INCLEMENT WEATHER ALL HIKERS MUST TAKE THE ALTERNATIVE ROUTES

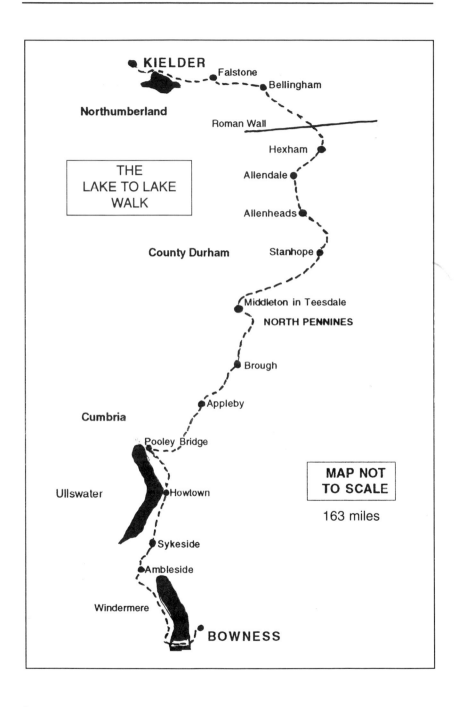

BOWNESS ON WINDERMERE

The town of Bowness stands midway along the eastern shore of Windermere.

As a starting point the town is an ideal choice. Close to motorway links and only a mile from Windermere Railway Station it enables easy access and at the same time the vast array of shops allows stocking up on the little essentials before the adventure begins.

The crowning glory of Bowness is of course Lake Windermere itself, a fitting point to start any walk. Throughout the passage of time the town of Bowness has always attracted tourists like moths to a flame; the Victorians revered this place, sampling the new steamboat trips up and down the lake, an enjoyment still experienced by visitors today.

Hikers generally regard the town as somewhere to avoid. The incessant arrival of coaches packed with day trippers makes Bowness one of, if not the, busiest town in the Lake District. To treat this welcoming town in such a manner is somewhat unfair. Whilst the throngs of people may hog the tourist oriented pubs sanity is but a short walk up Brantfell Road at the Royal Oak.

Traditionally and very romantically many writers start and finish long distance walks by suggesting you 'dip your toe in the lake or sea' and if this is what you want to do then please do so. For me, I would rather be wet on the inside than outside and so I have made the Royal Oak the official starting point for *The Lake to Lake*. Here a register is held for all hikers venturing out and if you would like to receive a memento of the walk please remember to sign it before setting off. After signing in at the end of the walk a certificate (for lunacy) will be forwarded to you free of charge.

On the night prior to your adventure there can be no better way of spending it than in the convivial atmosphere of the Royal Oak. Such is the popularity of this pub it is advisable to make your reservation as soon as possible.

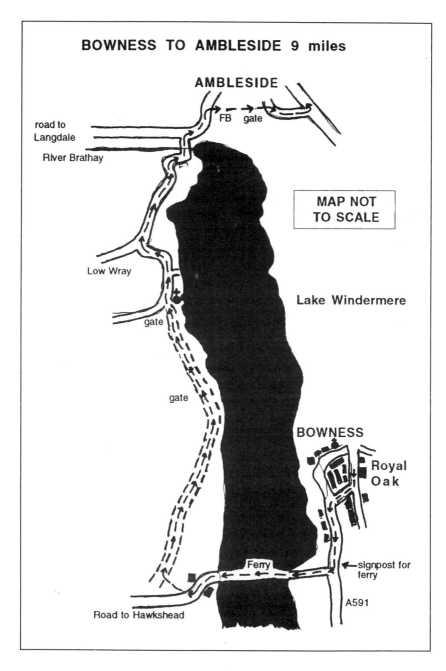

BOWNESS TO AMBLESIDE 9 miles

AMBLESIDE

road to
Langdale

FB   gate

River Brathay

MAP NOT
TO SCALE

Low Wray

Lake Windermere

gate

gate

BOWNESS

Royal
Oak

Ferry

signpost for
ferry

A591

Road to Hawkshead

BOWNESS TO AMBLESIDE

9 miles / 15.2 Km

The initial stages of the walk contain sections of road walking. Whilst this is unfortunate it is unavoidable so please take great care. Open country dominates the walk after Ambleside.

The Royal Oak, Bowness

On leaving The Royal Oak turn left up Brantfell Road and after approximately 100 yards turn right next to the Cranleigh Hotel, where the road sign informs you 'Car Ferry 1 mile'. Follow the road to the junction with the main road and turn left.

Follow this busy road until a turning on the right, signposted 'Hawkshead, Coniston B5285', leads down to the car and passenger ferry.

Cross the lake via the ferry and then follow the road for 200 yards before turning right onto the footpath. Soon a gate is met go through and turn right along the access road.

Continue along this easy to follow track which leads along the western shore of Windermere until eventually a footpath sign for 'High Wray' is found. Maintain this course alongside the lake.

As a gateway flanked by two stone pillars is passed through the route bends gently to the right, signposted 'Low Wray', and leads to a gate (ignore the stile on the left).

By maintaining this route another gate is soon reached. Follow the track directly ahead which in turn culminates at a meeting with the road where the gatehouse to Wray Castle can be seen to the right.

The Gatehouse to Wray Castle

At this point turn right following the road (unfortunate but there is no alternative) past the entrance to Low Wray campsite and onward to the junction, at which turn right.

Pass the mock Tudor building on your right and as the bend in the road is negotiated a permissive footpath on your right is taken. This runs parallel with the road and comes to an end at the stone staircase. Soon another path on the right is taken, again following the line of the road. As this path ends cross the road where a footpath sign reads 'permissive path to Ambleside'. Follow this to its conclusion on the banks of the river Brathay. Turn right along the side of the river and cross the old stone bridge, which leads up to the junction. Turn right.

Follow the line of the road until just prior to Ambleside where a footpath off to the right leads across a wooden footbridge, Go straight ahead at the gate, 'permissive path to Ambleside', and follow this to its conclusion on the banks of the river Brathay. Turn right along the side of the river and cross the old stone bridge, which leads up to the junction. Turn right.

FACILITIES ON THIS SECTION

After leaving Bowness there is nothing at all until you reach Ambleside.

The Waterwheel, Ambleside

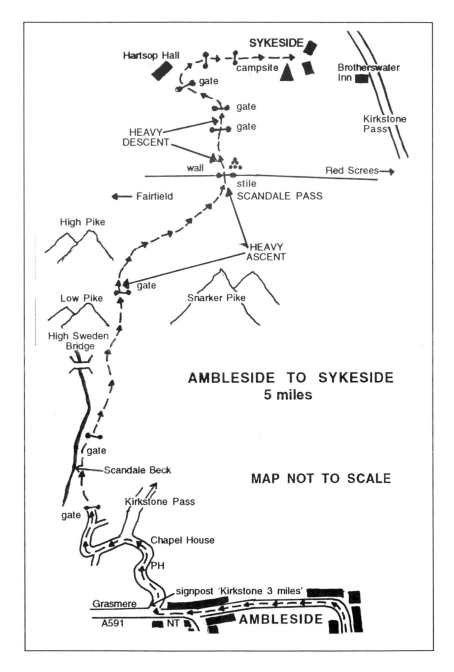

SYKESIDE

Hartsop Hall

campsite

Brotherswater Inn

gate

Kirkstone Pass

gate

gate

HEAVY DESCENT

wall

Red Screens →

stile
SCANDALE PASS

← Fairfield

HEAVY ASCENT

High Pike

gate

Low Pike

Snarker Pike

High Sweden Bridge

AMBLESIDE TO SYKESIDE
5 miles

gate

Scandale Beck

MAP NOT TO SCALE

Kirkstone Pass

gate

Chapel House

PH

signpost 'Kirkstone 3 miles'

Grasmere

A591   NT

AMBLESIDE

AMBLESIDE TO SYKESIDE

5 miles / 8 Km

After the rigours of the unavoidable road walk just encountered, the walk now begins in earnest and heads into open fell country.

From the centre of Ambleside follow the main Grasmere road out of the town. Passing the old National Trust House which spans the river, a turning on the right, signposted 'Kirkstone 3 miles', is taken, which in turn leads uphill past the Golden Rule public house. Follow the road as it swings left and reaches Chapel House on the right. Turn left at the signpost for 'Sweden Bridge Lane', follow this quiet back road ignoring a sign on the left for Belle Vue Lane and Low Sweden Bridge, instead continuing straight ahead. Maintain the steady climb and stay on this road all the way, ignoring all other turnings.

Eventually as a corner is turned a large gate can be seen directly ahead up the earthy track. Go through this gate and you are now heading into open country, at last. Follow this wall enclosed stony path all the way as it steadily climbs away from the confines of Ambleside, pausing only for the superb views across the valley as you go.

Soon the route starts a disconcerting drop as it enters woodland. Go through the gate and continue to follow this well trodden bridleway. To the left is the busy Scandale Beck. As the route continues to climb through the trees take great care as a series of sharp drops into the deep gorge appear without warning. Eventually the magnificent Sweden Bridge, an idyllic spot for a breather, is reached.

Without crossing the bridge bear right and follow the distinctive track. With Snarker Pike to the right and High Pike to the left this intimidating walk leads through a bowl to the base of Scandale at which a gate is passed through, and the climb begins. The way is self evident and gradually snakes around to the right. As the summit is thankfully reached a massive stile is clambered over.

At this point you are at the crossroads of two paths. To the right is the route up Red Screes and Middle Dodd, to the left the way to Fairfield and Helvellyn. Our route continues straight ahead on a barely visible path which is about ten yards to the right of the stile and immediately starts the descent. Beware, for the path ahead is treacherous to say the least. Even in dry weather the craggy terrain commands respect, in wet weather it is simply dangerous.

The path down continues to disappear regularly. However, by keeping the stream approximately twenty yards to your right the correct line is being followed. After half a mile negotiating the descent a small white building can be seen nestling in the pass below. This is the Brotherswater Inn and although you can see it, it takes quite a while before it starts to appear any larger. The steep descent finally abate alongside a stone wall where a pair of gates are passed through before reaching an old barn and another gate. Once again continue straight ahead, through the kissing gate and across the field towards the camp site. Cross the wooden footbridge and follow round to the old farm buildings and through the gate in the wall. Turn right and follow the track to the right into Sykeside.

The Brotherswater Inn, Kirkstone Pass

FACILITIES ON THIS SECTION

The town of Ambleside is one of the busiest in the Lake District and caters for all needs. It may be advisable to re-stock here as there is nothing else until Sykeside is reached.

SYKESIDE

On reaching the sanctuary of the Sykeside complex after a strenuous day it will be refreshing to know that this evening your accommodation, whether it be the campsite, the bunkhouse or even B&B in the Brotherswater Inn will be of the highest standards.

For many years now Sykeside has been a regular haunt of serious mountaineers, hikers and climbers, the surrounding hills providing a superb backdrop for what I personally consider to be the finest site in the whole of Lakeland.

Accommodation is available in the Brotherswater Pub, where evening meals are also served. A cheaper alternative is the bunkhouse, where cooking facilities are available or for the more hardy the peaceful campsite beckons. Whichever type of accommodation you choose, breakfasts are still available in the pub.

As an alternative to the Brotherswater you may wish to visit The Barn the other pub on the site, where seasoned hikers tend to gather and compare notes over a pint or two of the local real ale.

The complex also includes showers, laundry and a well stocked camp shop, where it is advised you replenish stocks before venturing out onto day two, as there are no facilities of note between here and Pooley Bridge.

Sykeside is a superb complex, I can think of no other word to describe it and it is so refreshing for a backpacker to know that they are not going to be kept awake by self centred visitors making merry throughout the night. Such behaviour is very swiftly dealt with.

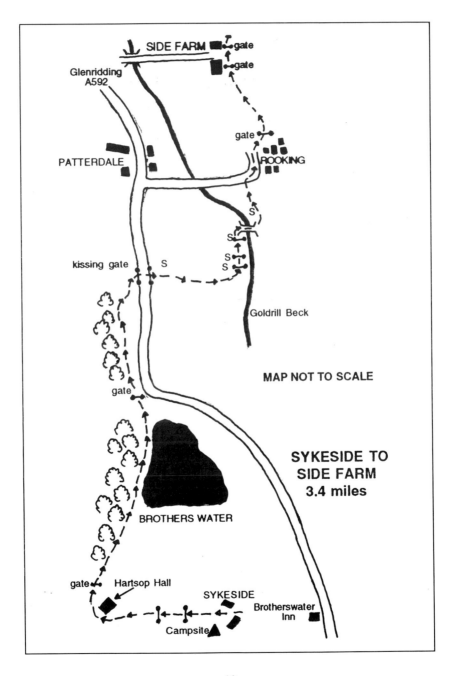

SIDE FARM
gate
gate

Glenridding
A592

gate

PATTERDALE

ROOKING

S

S
S
S

kissing gate   S

Goldrill Beck

gate

MAP NOT TO SCALE

SYKESIDE TO
SIDE FARM
3.4 miles

BROTHERS WATER

gate   Hartsop Hall

SYKESIDE

Brotherswater
Inn

Campsite

SYKESIDE TO SIDE FARM

3.4 miles / 5.5 Km

Please note that after leaving Sykeside there are no facilities whatsoever regarding food until Pooley Bridge is reached 15 miles hence. It is therefore advisable to restock at the campsite shop before venturing out. From the grounds of the Sykeside complex head due west across the campsite towards the gate and cattle grid directly ahead.

Continue on across the footbridge towards the farmhouse, through another gate and bear right around the back of the house through the gate and onto the well defined footpath. A pleasant stroll along the western bank of Brotherswater Lake ensues. Eventually a gate is reached where a signpost points the way for the 'permissive path to Patterdale'.

Follow this route to the left of the wall and with fence to your right. The route now enters woodland which is enjoyed as the path gently meanders its way to a kissing gate and a meeting with the road. Cross the road and go over the stile opposite at which point the path runs alongside Goldrill Beck. After passing two more stiles the path becomes a much wider track. Once again route finding along this section is straightforward and should cause no problems.

Soon another stile is crossed next to the wooden bridge. Cross the bridge and swing left as the track begins a short climb. At the top of the rise a triple signpost awaits. Take the trail to the left past the small farm building to the gate. As you approach the white house the walk mounts a few steps and follows around to a stile. Follow the track down and across the wooden footbridge and metal stile. Once over the stile turn right. This leads past the superb cottages at Rooking where the track is suddenly transformed into tarmac.

To the left can be seen the White Lion in Patterdale, a hostelry which throughout the years has become very popular with seasoned hikers and climbers. Soon another signpost directs you for Side Farm. After a short climb you will see yet another signpost, this time saying 'Angle Tarn'.

Rooking Cottage, Nr. Patterdale

Ignore this and pass through the large wooden gate to the left. This bridle way now leads directly to Side Farm. As you reach the farm go through the gate behind the farmhouse and continue straight ahead following the signpost for 'Howtown & Sandwick'.

FACILITIES ON THIS SECTION

As previously stated there are few facilities of note after leaving the Sykeside complex. On reaching Side Farm (depending on what time of year you visit) there is a possibility of refreshment. If you turn left between the farm buildings and look to your right there is a small café which has been created in one of the former farm buildings. This family run business serves up teas and coffees as well as snacks but is only open during the summer months. Although not applicable to this adventure you may be interested to know, for future jaunts, that Side Farm also offers a campsite. Although the pitches are generally sloping the price has been set accordingly and with a shower available next to the farm house this site provides good value for money. On the down side, if you want a pint on an evening you have a long walk back into Patterdale, as the White Lion is the nearest pub.

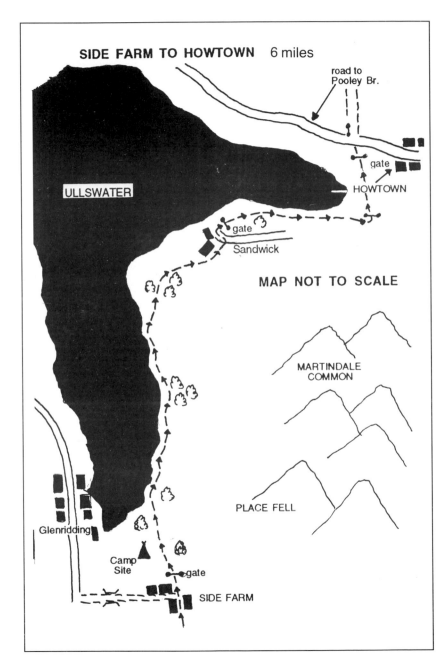

SIDE FARM TO HOWTOWN 6 miles

road to Pooley Br.

ULLSWATER

gate

HOWTOWN

gate

Sandwick

MAP NOT TO SCALE

MARTINDALE COMMON

PLACE FELL

Glenridding

Camp Site

gate

SIDE FARM

SIDE FARM TO HOWTOWN

6 miles / 9.7 Km

Known locally as 'the granny trot' the name falsely implies an easy walk suitable for almost anyone and is probably the reason why the rescue teams get called out to this area on a regular basis. Whilst at first sight the map implies a pleasant lakeside stroll the reality is a never ending rollercoaster of a walk over unearthed tree roots and loose boulders.

Proceed through the gate at the rear of Side Farm and continue along the wall enclosed bridleway. Eventually the path opens out as the camp site is passed. Route finding is extremely easy along this section and the magnificent sight of Ullswater to your left can be enjoyed throughout the section. After an undulating trek the route begins the descent into the tiny and somewhat idyllic hamlet of Sandwick. As the cottages are reached at the tarmac road turn left and continue to the bottom of the hill where a stone signpost (footpath to Howtown) directs you to the right, through the wooden gate. Follow the bridleway all the way, taking great care as the unearthed tree roots already mentioned in this section become more evident. As the headland on the approach to Howtown is rounded a kissing gate on the left is found. Go through this gate and descend the man made staircase, which leads directly into the village of Howtown. Pass the landing stage for the Ullswater ferry and continue up to join the road.

HOWTOWN

A place many people especially from the north of England can identify with. The Outward Bound Centre, once owned by Durham County Council, has accommodated thousands of children over many years on courses which have helped to build character and introduce future hikers and climbers to the wonders of the great outdoors.

FACILITIES ON THIS SECTION

None until arrival in Howtown where there is a well appointed pub.

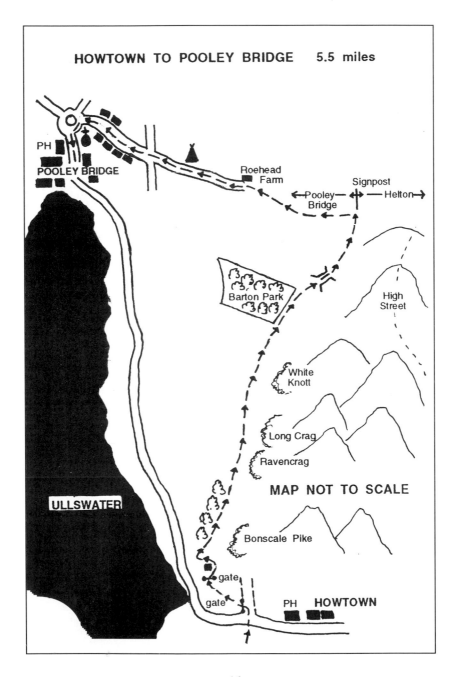

HOWTOWN TO POOLEY BRIDGE 5.5 miles

PH

POOLEY BRIDGE

Roehead Farm

Signpost

←— Pooley —← →— Helton —→
Bridge

Barton Park

High Street

White Knott

Long Crag

Ravencrag

MAP NOT TO SCALE

Bonscale Pike

ULLSWATER

gate

gate

PH HOWTOWN

HOWTOWN TO POOLEY BRIDGE

5.5 miles / 8.9 Km

On reaching the landing stage for the Lake Ferry continue straight ahead to reach the road.

Directly ahead can be seen the access road for the Outdoor Centre and just to the left a gate leading into a field. Go through the gate and bear diagonally right up the field to reach a gate at the top. Once through proceed through the next gate directly ahead.

The route then swings left and passes a static caravan as it starts to gently climb up the old track. Route finding along this well used bridle way is self evident and soon, after passing a small copse to your left, the path reaches open fell. High to your right, as the way continues to climb, can be seen the daunting crags of Bonscale Pike, Raven Crag and Auterstone Crag.

By this point the views across Ullswater to the left are superb and make the long haul well worthwhile. Shortly after passing the covers of an underground reservoir a tree plantation on the left is passed at the end of which a signpost is to be found which states 'Pooley Bridge 1.75 miles' (someone cannot measure distances, it is actually 2.75). A short downhill stretch leads across the stream at the bridge and continues to follow the bridle way, again very easy route finding.

Continue to follow the bridle way which soon meets up with one of the nicest walks in the Lake District, High Street, and within half a mile a signpost informs you that Helton is to the right and Pooley Bridge to the left, where a decision is to be made.

If you intend to stay overnight in Pooley Bridge, and please note that if you do so you will have to retrace your steps back to this signpost the following morning, then turn left and follow the bridle way downhill. This soon becomes a track and then a tarmac access road. On reaching the cross-roads continue straight ahead to arrive at a small roundabout from which a left turn leads into the heart of this small yet attractive village.

If you do not intend to stay in Pooley Bridge then turn right and refer to the next section.

The Sun Inn, Pooley Bridge

FACILITIES ON THIS SECTION

There is a pub in Howtown but after that there is absolutely nothing until Pooley Bridge is reached. It should also be noted that after Pooley Bridge there are no facilities until Newby (11 miles away). Pooley Bridge will forever hold a special place in my heart for it is here I first had the chance to pass on the benefit of my thirty years in the hills to a group of children, children for many of whom it would be their first chance to discover the wonders of the Lake District.

POOLEY BRIDGE

A popular haunt of the dreaded four wheeled day tripper, this attractive settlement at the northern end of Ullswater provides good hospitality for an overnight stay. Pubs seem to dominate the village (shame) with more than its fair share. The shops are well stocked and accommodation is plentiful. Pooley Bridge also offers a choice of campsites, two of which are well out of the immediate vicinity; the nearest to all amenities however is situated enroute just prior to reaching the cross-roads on the approach to the village.

THE DURHAM YOUTH ENTEPRISE SCHEME

Researching, plotting and writing books such as the one you are now using take a considerable amount of time and it becomes very easy to bury yourself in your work and not fully appreciate the undoubted benefits you get from spending so much time in the beautiful scenic areas of the world.

In the summer of 1999 my daughter Heather was nominated by her school for a five day course in the Lake District. During this course she would be abseiling, hiking, mountain biking, canoeing and doing a host of other activities. As a parent I asked the obvious question, 'How much'? I was amazed when she answered, 'It's free'. On further investigation I discovered The Durham Youth Enterprise Scheme, a scheme which has been set up to reward children for achievement whether social, academic or whatever.

The scheme caters for more than 120 children each summer and survives thanks not only to a National Lottery Grant but to the time and effort of other bodies such as The Prince's Trust, Durham Constabulary, Durham and Frankland Prisons and a host of private businesses.

The courses are run by qualified instructors and a number of group leaders all of whom give their time free of charge and I was particularly honoured when I was asked if I would consider being the Fell Instructor.

Based at Park Foot Campsite in Pooley Bridge the participants spend five days learning not only about the great outdoors and sleeping under canvas but also having courses on drugs awareness and community projects. For many it is the first time away from parents. Others, who are not so lucky, have no parents.

Instructing on the D.Y.E.S was an enlightening experience for me. Although approached with trepidation the project was something I will cherish for the rest of my life. In the pages that follow and as a tribute to both the staff and the participants of the scheme I have included a number of photographs which I hope in some small way capture the whole meaning. Should you wish to get any more information on this scheme then please contact me personally through my publisher.

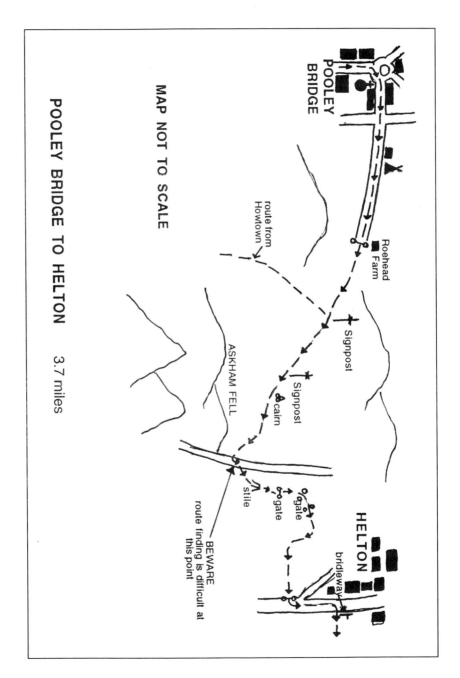

POOLEY
BRIDGE

Roehead
Farm

route from
Howtown

Signpost

ASKHAM FELL

Signpost

cairn

stile

gate

gate

BEWARE
route finding is difficult at
this point

HELTON

bridleway

MAP NOT TO SCALE

POOLEY BRIDGE TO HELTON   3.7 miles

POOLEY BRIDGE TO HELTON

3.7 miles / 6 Km

For walkers who have taken the opportunity to stay in Pooley Bridge overnight retrace your steps back up the access road, past Roehead Farm and up the bridleway to the sign post mentioned previously.

Bridleway signpost on Askham Fell

On reaching the signpost, as shown, follow the direction indicator for 'Helton', that is, straight ahead for walkers coming from Pooley Bridge and a right turn for walkers coming from Howtown.

Continue up this easy to follow way as it rises gently, taking time to turn and bid a fond and, as always with this area, a sad farewell to the Lakeland Fells. Soon another signpost is reached, again follow the sign indicator for 'Helton' which is straight ahead. The wide expanse of open fell country now being crossed is the often bleak and windswept top of Askham Fell. Follow this well trodden bridleway for another mile until a road is somewhat surprisingly and no doubt reluctantly met.

Go to the road and turn left, walk up the road for only approximately eighty yards where a faint green path leads off to the right. Take great care in route finding at this point as the path is not easy to determine. Within yards you will know if you have found the trail by looking directly ahead. You should see a dry stone wall and a large stile surmounting it. Continue to the stile.

The first major contrast of this trek is now about to take place. After the rugged and demanding terrain of the Lakeland peaks the walk is now entering a Dales like phase as it passes through the Eden valley. Once over the stile continue across the field bearing slightly left to arrive at a gate in the far left corner. Go through the gate and, keeping the wall to your left head down the field to the gate at the bottom. Once through this gate you are now on a wall enclosed path, follow this as it swings right and then sharply left to arrive at the road. Once at the road turn left and continue along the side of this road until the first house in the tiny hamlet of Helton is reached. At this point a signpost to the right, 'Public Bridleway to Whale' is met.

Turn right down this enclosed way.

FACILITIES ON THIS SECTION

After leaving the rather hectic surroundings of Pooley Bridge there is nothing at all in the way of facilities along this section. It is therefore advisable to stock up before setting off. The next port of call for possible refreshments is at Newby (and that is only at the hotel).

HANDY HINTS

For the less experienced hiker it is often beneficial to hear of the lessons learned by others. Throughout the rest of the book, where space allows, I will be passing on some of the more important lessons I have learned during my career. Many will seem obvious, but often too easily ignored.

Here is the first of them.

Many walkers in their formative years approach a climb in the same manner as they would a level walk, resulting in fatigue and continuous stops. By shortening your stride as you climb energy levels are not sapped and the summit reached without distress.

Participants on the DYES with the author

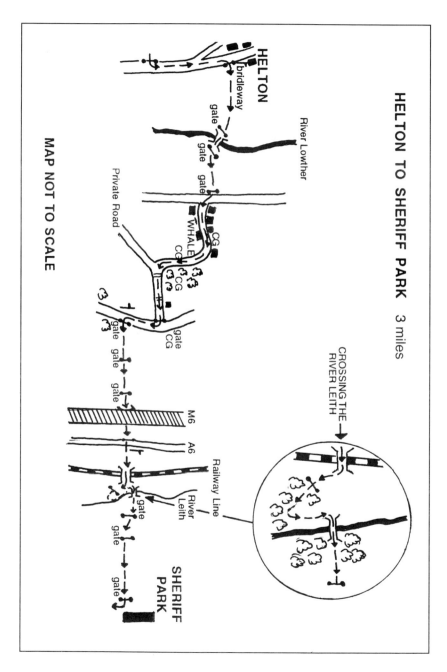

HELTON TO SHERIFF PARK   3 miles

MAP NOT TO SCALE

HELTON

bridleway

gate

gate

gate

gate

River Lowther

Private Road

WHALE

CG

CG

CG

gate
CG

gate

gate
CG

gate

gate

M6

A6

Railway Line

River
Leith

gate

gate

gate

gate

SHERIFF
PARK

CROSSING THE
RIVER LEITH

HELTON TO SHERIFF PARK

3 miles / 4.8 Km

Turning right onto the enclosed, and somewhat overgrown bridleway at Helton the route is self evident and culminates at a gate. Go through the gate and, as the way opens out from its confines, continue straight ahead, soon to arrive at a wooden footbridge on the left. Cross the bridge, which carries you over the River Lowther and through the gate, bend to the right and through another gate, at which point turn left, pass to the right of the tree and follow the path alongside the stream.

A short climb leads up to a gate and a meeting with the road. Continue directly ahead, that is up the road which is signposted 'Whale'. Pass through this sleepy hamlet following the road all the way until a farm is reached, bear right across the cattle grid and continue to follow this access road past the wall enclosed copse on your left. Pass over two more cattle grids and soon a junction of roads is reached. At this point turn left, once again restricted to the access road and pass a barn to the left. This seemingly never ending road eventually terminates at a gate. Turn right across the cattle grid and continue up the road, ignore a sign for 'Hackthorpe' to your left and maintain a route directly ahead. In the distance can be seen the obnoxious sight of traffic hurtling up and down the M6, poor misguided souls.

As a second cattle grid is reached the road is thankfully vacated, a Public Bridleway sign to the right can be seen. Ignore this and turn left through the gate, continue along the side of the fence until a metal gate is reached at the far end of the field. Go through the gate and start the tree enclosed climb to the gate at the top. By keeping to the right and following the edge of the field the underpass is soon seen. Pass under the M6, continue up the track directly ahead to a gate and arrival at a road.

Cross straight over the road, through the gate, where a signpost says 'Public Bridleway, Sheriff Park', and, as the path is indistinguishable, follow exactly the line of the direction marker. This leads across a field to a gate and crosses the bridge over the railway line.

Once over the bridge turn sharply right along the side of the fence. After approximately 50 yards start to bear left across the field to a gate in the far left hand corner. Go through the gate and start to head downhill through the dense copse.

Once the stream (River Leith) is reached way finding becomes difficult. Basically ignore the sign and turn left; after 50 yards a wooden footbridge is crossed. Continue directly ahead which leads up a short but very demanding incline to rejoin the bridleway.

As the top of the climb is reached a large gate looms ahead. Bear to the left and go through the smaller gate. Once through, follow the line of the fence to the next gate. Continue on until the boundary fence to the houses at Sheriff Park is reached. At this point turn acutely right and proceed to the next gate.

Looking back to Sheriff Park

FACILITIES ON THIS SECTION

None whatsoever.

The author with fellow instructors from the DYES

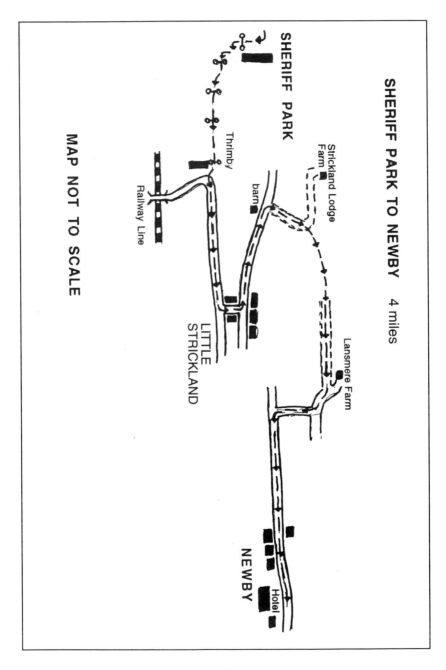

SHERIFF PARK

SHERIFF PARK TO NEWBY   4 miles

MAP NOT TO SCALE

Thrimby

Strickland Lodge Farm

barn

Railway Line

LITTLE STRICKLAND

Lansmere Farm

NEWBY

Hotel

SHERIFF PARK TO NEWBY

4 miles / 6.4 Km

Having turned sharply right at the boundary fence of the houses at Sheriff Park go through the gate and follow around the left edge of the field to a gate in the far corner. Proceed along the edge of the ensuing field to another gate, the bridleway clearly defined. Follow this to yet another gate and once through bear right.

The route now passes under the pylons and continues all the way to the small cluster of houses at Thrimby. As the road is reached turn left and follow the narrow enclosed country lane all the way to Little Strickland.

Turn left at the first turning in the village, signposted 'Great Strickland', continue up the road for only a matter of 50 yards and then turn left again. At this point you have almost turned 180 degrees and appear to be heading back the way you came; unfortunately this short reversal cannot be avoided.

Climb the hill ahead and continue to follow the road so that you are almost level with the houses at Thrimby on the road below. At the top of the hill a disused barn on the left marks the end of road walking. Turn right at this point (signposted 'Public Bridleway - Stonehills') for 'Strickland Lodge'.

Follow the track and pass through the gate, As the track bends to the left towards the farmhouse our route continues directly ahead running parallel with the wall on your right, which in turn leads to a gate. Continue up the field, through another gate. Soon the wall comes to an end. Maintain your direction straight ahead where a gate can be seen in the near distance.

Keep following the track, another of those that seems never ending but it does eventually emerge at a gravel road, bear right and continue along the road for a few yards before turning right and past the ever so picturesque rubbish tip. The track emerges at the road where a left turn is made, which leads directly into the superb hamlet of Newby.

FACILITIES ON THIS SECTION

For the first time since Pooley Bridge facilities present themselves, well almost, in the tiny hamlet of Newby. With only the hotel servicing needs choice is strictly limited; however read on to discover the delights of this establishment.

NEWBY

On any long distance walk villages and towns are regularly visited. Often we pass through and never really give them a second glance. Newby however commands a special mention.

Even as the first house in this small community is passed the visitor can begin to realise that they are entering a village where the local residents care about their surroundings and image. Litter free (even the public telephone box is regularly cleaned by one of the locals) and well cared for properties make Newby a place which typifies everything that is good in rural England. Facilities are minimal. There is a farm shop which only opens two afternoons per week but the gem which makes this place so special is the fabulous Newby Hall.

The Newby Hall Hotel

Thought to be built on the site of the former home of mediaeval knight, Roger de Newby, this magnificent Tudor built mansion now acts as a privately run hotel, which also welcomes with open arms non residential customers. Full of atmosphere, the hotel and its staff are very welcoming. The accommodation is good, a range of real ales and weekly guest ales await your palate whilst sustenance in the form of food can be obtained in either the excellent restaurant or simply as a bar meal. Packed lunches for the following day can also be purchased.

As a backpacker I was especially pleased to see that provision had been made for such hardy souls at the rear of the Hotel. This may only be a plot of grass and a tap but what more do we need?

HANDY HINTS

The one advantage backpackers have is that they are carrying everything they need to survive the expedition. That means that if they are in desperate need of a cuppa they can stop and put on a brew, especially thankful on a long section as just covered with no facilities.

By also carrying a flask you can avoid having to drink the tainted tea or coffee that comes out of them and also save on a precious commodity for any backpacker, gas. On leaving the previous night's camp fill the flask with warm or hot water. When you want a brew pour the water into your billy and reheat. The tea will taste much better and your gas supplies will be preserved.

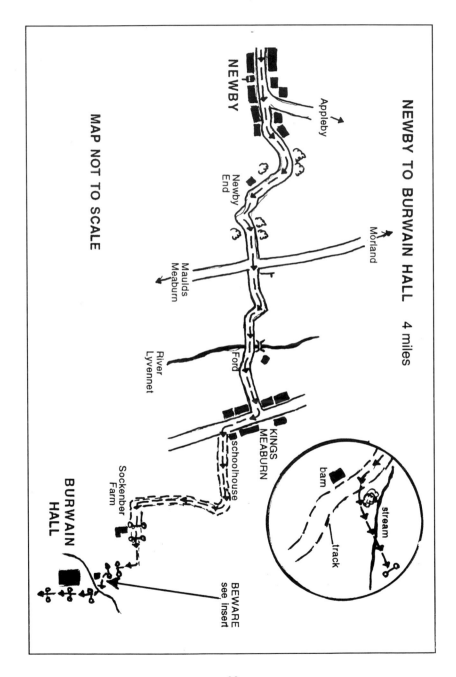

NEWBY TO BURWAIN HALL   4 miles

MAP NOT TO SCALE

NEWBY

Appleby

Morland

Newby
End

Maulds
Meaburn

River
Lyvennet

Ford

KINGS
MEABURN

schoolhouse

Sockenber
Farm

BURWAIN
HALL

BEWARE
see insert

barn

stream

track

NEWBY TO BURWAIN HALL

4 miles / 6.8 Km

The following section contains a good deal of road walking. Whilst this is never ideal the pleasant accompanying scenery as we head down the Eden Valley make it none-the-less an enjoyable and worthwhile experience.

Continue along the road through the village, passing the telephone box and as the road swings sharply to the left (signposted Morland and Appleby) our route proceeds straight ahead (for Maulds Meaburn).

This quiet back road is now followed, making route finding simple and allowing time to enjoy the flora and fauna that abound along the road side. As a cross-roads is reached the route continues straight ahead. In the far distance can be seen the awesome and beckoning Pennines, which eagerly await your arrival.

The road eventually starts to drop steeply and arrives at a splendidly picturesque ford, where a somewhat rickety footbridge crosses the river Lyvennet.

The bridge at King's Meaburn

Once over the bridge continue straight ahead up the steep incline to arrive in the village of Kings Meaburn.

At the junction turn right and again following the road, proceed to the end of the village where a left turn is made next to the tiny old schoolhouse. This is signposted 'Public Bridleway - Burwain Hall', and is no doubt a relief after the past few miles of road walking.

The route follows the bridleway and as the bottom of the hill is reached the route swings sharply right as a gate is almost reached. This track continues in a direct line until the end of the caravan site on the right. At this point turn left and proceed to climb the hill ahead.

After a daunting climb a farmhouse on the right is passed. Continue straight ahead staying on the track. Go through one gate before reaching another two gates in quick succession.

At the second gate you will also see another gate to your right. Ignore this and go through the wooden gate directly ahead; this leads onto an enclosed way which, after 100 yards swings right.

As this enclosed path comes to an end a gate is reached. Go through and proceed stright ahead to the next gate. Maintain your route along this path until you are within 20 yards of a barn on your right.

From this point take great care as route finding is hazardous.

Just as the track starts to turn right to pass the barn vacate it and bear left down to the stream which can be seen below. Cross the stream and bear right up the very faint footpath to arrive at a gate in a dry stone wall. Once through the gate continue along the side of the fence to another gate. By maintaining this line up the side of the fence another gate is passed through before arriving at the access track at Burwain Hall, which can be seen on the right.

FACILITIES ON THIS SECTION

None whatsoever in relation to refreshment but there is a public telephone box in the hamlet of King's Meaburn.

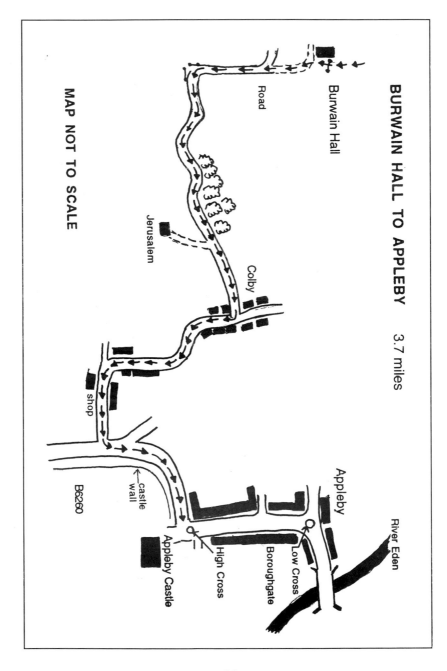

BURWAIN HALL TO APPLEBY   3.7 miles

MAP NOT TO SCALE

Burwain Hall

Road

Jerusalem

Colby

shop

B6260

castle wall

Appleby Castle

High Cross

Boroughgate

Low Cross

Appleby

River Eden

BURWAIN HALL TO APPLEBY

3.7 miles / 6 Km

The following section is 90% road walking, which although not ideal, does make for easy route finding and allows time to enjoy the magnificent scenery of both the Eden Valley and the Pennines which surround you.

Once the gate has been reached with the rather drab and forboding Burwain Hall to your right, pass through and bear left onto the track. The track is followed all the way to its culmination at a junction with the road. At this point turn left and follow the road downhill. Soon it swings left and begins to rise and fall over the swells left by the remnants of glacial debris millions of years ago. As the road is followed the ever nearing Pennines now begin to loom large and provide an excellent backdrop for what is a long and energy sapping stretch of road walking.

Continue to follow the road, until, eventually, to your right, can be seen Jerusalem. Don't worry, you haven't taken a wrong turning, it is actually the name of a farm which can be seen nestling to the right. As the road finally, and thankfully reaches a junction in the small hamlet of Colby a right turn is made. This then follows through the village and starts a fairly heavy climb up the road. Take heart, for once at the top the town of Appleby is not far away.

Continue to follow the road and as the outskirts of the proud town of Appleby in Westmorland are passed the road swings left, past a corner shop on the right, to arrive at the main road. At this point turn left and cross this busy road. Follow this road up the hill, gradually bearing right alongside the castle wall to the top. To the right can be seen the entrance to Appleby Castle but by crossing the road once again and bearing left, the main thoroughfare through the town, Boroughgate, is joined. For information on accommodation and camping facilities, the Tourist Information Office is at the bottom of this road on the left.

FACILITIES ON THIS SECTION

There are no facilities whatsoever on this section until the market town of Appleby in Westmorland is reached, where the full range of amenities you would associate with a town of this size are available.

APPLEBY IN WESTMORLAND

Once the county town of the former county of Westmorland, the picturesque town of Appleby stands on a loop in the river in the heart of the Eden Valley. Sheltered by both the Pennines and the Lakeland Fells the town enjoys a milder climate than most of Cumbria and therefore is an extremely popular venue for holidaymakers.

Looking at the town today it is hard to understand that this bustling community was actually laid waste in 1388 by marauding bands of raiders from across the Scottish border. As Appleby was re-built the natural charm and character you see before you today was most certainly retained.

Entering the town from the south the daunting sight of the Norman Castle greets the inquisitive visitor. Built in AD 1174 the castle provides a perfect example of the 'Motte and Bailey' type of defensive construction, with a tall tower built within an encircling wall. The domestic buildings were originally added in the 14th century and were restored to their present state in 1688. Today the castle is private property. However the grounds which house the Rare Breeds Survival Trust and the Norman Keep, somewhat mysteriously named Caesar's Tower, are open to the public throughout the summer and well worth a visit.

One cannot help but be impressed by the monuments at either end of Boroughgate, which are known as the 'High' and 'Low' Crosses and mark the boundaries of the original markets. At the 'High' end would have been the cheese market whilst at the 'Low' the butter trade developed, and in between, traders would deal in cattle, pigs and a host of other related services. Behind the 'High' Cross can be seen the Cloisters and St. Lawrence's Church, final resting place of Lady

Anne Clifford who did so much in restoring Appleby in the 17th century. Other examples of Norman architecture, the church still retains are the mediaeval nave and antique organ.

A walk down Boroughgate reveals a host of fine architecture, a 17th century house, now a pharmacy and the Post Office bearing a 1653 datestone being fine examples of the delights Appleby has to offer. At the bottom of the hill is the 'Moot Hall', which now houses the Tourist Information Office and has been the site of town council meetings for many centuries. Originally the building was the Assize Court and remained so until 1770.

Turning right at the bottom of Boroughgate the old stone bridge, built in 1889, replacing the previous mediaeval one, leads across the tranquil River Eden where the traditional sight of English cricket can still be observed at the immaculately kept Cricket Club. Appleby is one of the busier places encountered on this walk and provides a good chance to recuperate and replenish supplies for the days ahead, whilst at the same time exploring the fascinating history the town has to offer.

APPLEBY HORSE FAIR

Without doubt mention the town of Appleby to someone and they will immediately identify it with the Horse Fair that has been held in the town for many centuries. Reputed to be the largest Fair of its kind in the world, visitors from many far flung places make an annual pilgrimage here each June to witness at first hand the racing and trading in horses conducted by the 'travelling people'.

The Fair is said to have existed under the protection of a charter given by King James II; however this statement can almost certainly be discounted when the history books are consulted. Indeed James II did grant a charter to Appleby in 1685, and it cannot be denied that this charter allowed for the trading of Goods, Cattle, Horses, Mares and Geldings. It is not until the timing of the market is looked at that discrepancies occur, for in the charter it states that the market will be held on the second Tuesday in April, not the first week in June as is the case.

Looking at the historical evidence it appears the origins of the Fair can be reliably traced to 1750, when the town's Mayor, Aldermen and Councillors gave permission for a June and September Fair to be held each year, therefore exploding the romantic myth that it was an ancient Royal Charter.

Although the origins of the Fair, or 'happening' as it is locally called, can be questioned there is no questioning the popularity of this annual get together. For many weeks and days before the fair begins the surrounding countryside and villages all play host to the numerous travellers as they make their way to Appleby. For many of them reaching Appleby will be the culmination of a long and sometimes arduous journey. The sight of so many varying forms of transport is a sight to behold, from the Gypsy Vados (horse drawn caravans) to the more usual palatial chromed vans towed by Range Rovers and even Rolls Royces. The never ending stream of visitors converge on this normally quiet Cumbrian town.

Throughout the week trading intensifies, stall holders do a brisk trade whilst from the bursting pubs can be heard the sound of violins and hearty singing. Over the years Appleby Horse Fair has been degraded by the media in general, non-stop fighting and drunken behaviour always seems to dominate the news, but the truth is that this Fair is an experience that everyone should sample. Where there is a large gathering of people you will always get disputes and yes, you will also find pickpockets etc. but that can apply to anywhere and Appleby Fair is no worse and no better than any other similar event. Some of the pubs do close down for the week but having talked to landlords who do remain open they confirm that skirmishes are few and far between and when they do happen they are sorted very quickly. Cumbria Police allocate two Police Officers to every pub for the duration of the Fair whose job it is to oversee behaviour in that particular establishment.

Appleby gives the visitor the opportunity to take a glimpse into the normally inaccessible world of the Gypsy travellers. Do not let the media taint your interest, judge for yourself by visiting this ancient festival.

FACILITIES AFTER LEAVING APPLEBY

Please note that the following section which takes us to Brough has no facilities at all. The route is more than 10 miles in length and therefore it is advisable to stock up before venturing out. In an emergency there are telephone boxes at Great Ormside, Sandford, Warcop and Little Musgrave.

The Lower Cross, Appleby

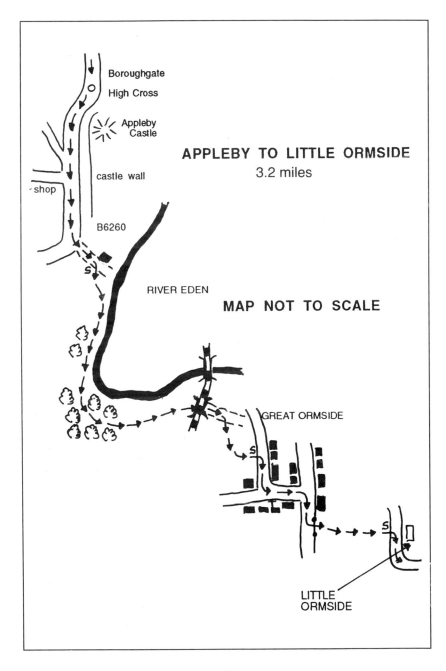

Boroughgate

High Cross

Appleby
Castle

castle wall

shop

B6260

S

RIVER EDEN

APPLEBY TO LITTLE ORMSIDE
3.2 miles

MAP NOT TO SCALE

GREAT ORMSIDE

S

S

LITTLE
ORMSIDE

APPLEBY TO LITTLE ORMSIDE

3.2 miles / 5.1 Km

To leave Appleby retrace your steps back to the top of Boroughgate and follow the road round to the right. When you reach the bottom of the hill, opposite the corner shop passed on the way into Appleby, continue straight ahead up the road, the B6260 alongside the castle wall and, as the top of the hill is reached and the road bends sharply to the right, take the track directly ahead.

This leads downhill to a signpost on the right, 'Public Footpath-Ormside'. Turn right through the kissing gate and onto the well defined footpath. This enclosed path leads to a stile. Cross and continue straight ahead, way finding remaining relatively easy at this point.

The River Eden at Warcop

The route continues alongside the River Eden. Soon another stile is crossed which in turn leads to a metal stile and into the woodland beyond. As the copse is negotiated a metal girder bridge is crossed before arriving at yet another stile. As this stile is crossed another copse can be seen directly ahead.

At this point head diagonally left across the field to a stile in the far corner. Continue through the wood and cross the small stream at the stepping stones. Go up to the stile and maintain your route along this well defined path along the riverbank.

As soon as the route leaves the river side a man made wooden staircase is climbed. On reaching the top the route bends round to the left and passes along the top side of the trees with the fence to your right. Proceed to the stile ahead which crosses the fence, bends to the left and crosses the wooden footbridge before gradually swinging right.

A short but formidable climb ensues, goes through the wood once again, along the side of the burn, and arrives at a stile. Continue the route along the side of the trees to arrive at a gate. Once through turn sharply left. This widened footpath then swings right to pass over a stile and under the railway bridge. Follow the track until a gate appears on the right. Turn right through this gate and cross the field where a stile is negotiated in the far left hand corner. Turn left and this leads to the road.

Once onto the road turn right and follow it for only 20 yards before turning left opposite the telephone box. Within another 20 yards turn right along the hedge-lined road and proceed for almost 100 yards where a sign says 'Public Footpath' to the left. Go through the gate and continue straight ahead, over a succession of three stiles to arrive at a gate.

Once through the next stile is slightly off to the left. Way markers make this an easy section to follow. Two more stiles follow before arriving at a gate which leads out onto a road. Turn right at this point and follow the road up to pass behind the farmhouse at Little Ormside.

FACILITIES ON THIS SECTION

Having left the comfort of Appleby there are no facilities along this section of the route. The next available place for supplies is Brough, 11.5 miles away.

For many years I have been accompanied on some of my jaunts by long term friend Dave Clough (centre). From time to time the tranquil nature of our treks is disturbed by the constant laughs provided by Ray Allinson (left) and Paul Reach (right).

Good Friends!

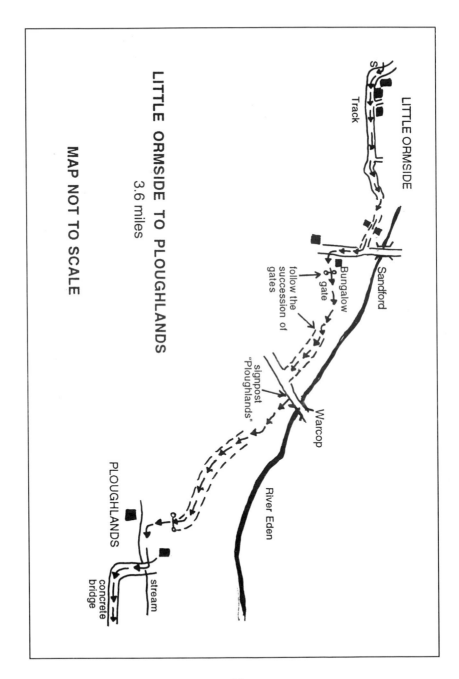

LITTLE ORMSIDE TO PLOUGHLANDS

3.6 miles

MAP NOT TO SCALE

LITTLE ORMSIDE TO PLOUGHLANDS

3.6 miles / 5.8 Km

Follow the road behind the farm and continue along the enclosed track, which continues for a considerable time until eventually two gates are reached. Ignoring the one off to the right continue straight ahead along the fainter yet still distinct track. Pass through a second gate. Soon the track starts to disintegrate as it passes the wood.

Continue along the side of the trees until two more gates are reached. Take the one to the left, which in turn, leads along a narrow path with the trees to the left and fence to the right. The path begins to drop down as it swings left to arrive at the farm at the bottom of the valley. Go through the gate and pass between the farm buildings and down the track. Cross the first bridge and proceed to the junction.

At this point another bridge can be seen to your left. Ignore this and turn right, passing the bungalow on your left. Then turn left through the gate and proceed to climb up the right side of the field keeping the hedgerow to your right to reach the gate at the top. Go through the gate and now with the hedgerow on your left another gate is passed through. Keep next to the hedge on the left and the correct route will be followed.

Continue through a gap in the hedgerow ahead ignoring an old gate on your left and continuing down to a gate in the corner of the field. This leads onto a track. Follow the main track which swings left to a gate and an enclosed footpath. Continue along the path, ignoring a gate which appears on the right until the path widens and to the left appears the village of Warcop.

Keep following the track and at the bottom turn right. This follows the banks of the River Eden and leads to the road. On reaching the road turn left and, just prior to crossing the bridge, a footpath sign is found on the right saying 'Ploughlands'. Turn right at this point and once again follow along the pleasant trail parallel with the river. Eventually a gate is reached. Continue straight ahead, ignoring the stile on the left, and follow the track which starts to rise high above the Eden. The path runs along the side of the fence to a double pair of gates. Once again continue straight ahead maintaining a steady climb as the route starts to leave the river. After the crest is reached the farm at Ploughlands can now be seen. Proceed through a pair of gates and follow down the side of the hedgerow. Ignore a gate on the left and continue to the gate directly ahead. Once through turn sharply left, without crossing the stream. Cross the little stone footbridge and over the stile and onto the farm access at Ploughlands.

FACILITIES ON THIS SECTION

As previously pointed out, there are no facilities on this section although a short detour to either Sandford or Warcop can be made.

HANDY HINTS

Backpacking, although giving a certain amount of autonomy, also provides a few problems for the inexperienced hiker.

Keeping equipment clean is an essential part of any expedition whether in the English hills, the Alps or even the Himalayas. The most essential items to be kept clean are the cooking utensils. An unclean pan can lead to all manner of problems and with a multi-day trek ahead the last thing you want is a bad case of 'fell runs'.

Carrying Fairy Liquid and pan scourers is obviously not practical but, in fact, you have all the cleaning products you need near at hand. A couple of pieces of fern make an excellent scourer. For more stubborn stains put some very small pieces of shingle from a river bed into the pan, add a modicum of water and swirl - as good as any scouring pad.

Preparing for the night

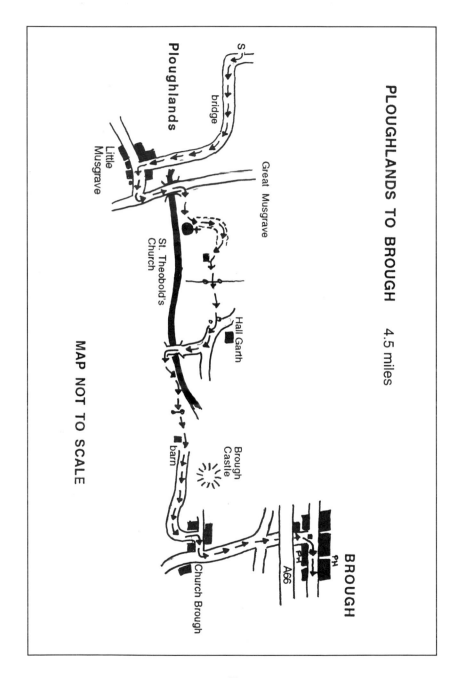

PLOUGHLANDS TO BROUGH   4.5 miles

MAP NOT TO SCALE

Ploughlands

bridge

Little
Musgrave

Great Musgrave

St. Theobold's
Church

Hall Garth

barn

Brough
Castle

Church Brough

A66

PH

PH

BROUGH

PLOUGHLANDS TO BROUGH

4.5 miles / 6.4 Km

Having turned right after crossing the stile now follow the concrete access road as it swings to the left and over the bridge. Stay on this road all the way, soon to cross the cattle grid. The track seems to go on for an eternity but eventually it terminates as another cattle grid is crossed and the road reached in the tiny hamlet of Little Musgrave.

Turn left at the road and follow this road past the telephone box all the way to a junction at the end of the lane. There is a signpost for a public footpath to Musgrave Bridge to your left as Little Musgrave is left, but ignore this as it leads to absolutely nowhere. Once at the road junction turn left and follow the road for a short journey to cross the bridge.

After crossing the bridge take the footpath off to your right, signposted 'St. Theobold's Church'. This proceeds parallel with the river for a short distance before arriving at the church where a gate is passed through. Turn left at the signpost 'Public Bridleway - Great Musgrave'. This winding and steep tarmac path is climbed. At the top as the houses are passed a sign is found, 'Public Footpath- Hallgarth'; turn right at this point, proceed through the double iron gates and turn immediately left, cross the pasture to the edge of the stone wall and then directly ahead can be seen two iron gates, in the centre of which is a stile. Cross the stile and continue directly ahead, through the gap in the clump of trees and towards the farm at the bottom of the field. Go through the gate and turn right.

Follow this road for a short distance and turn right again across the bridge and turn left at the public footpath sign. Follow the path directly ahead. Soon another gate is reached, the path swings left and then right and proceeds to a gate at the top of a short rise. Proceed straight across the field, to a gate half way up. Ahead can be seen the barn where another gate leading out onto a wider track is taken. Follow this track all the way. To the left can be seen the remains of Brough Castle.

Finally the road starts to sweep left and climbs to reach the houses at

Church Brough. Turn right and then left onto the road which leads downhill, past the school and under the bridge which carries traffic on the busy and infamous A66. Soon the centre of Brough is reached at a junction next to the Clock Tower. Turn right.

FACILITIES ON THIS SECTION

After the walk from Appleby you will no doubt be in need of sustenance. Although there have been no facilities along this section (unless you diverted into Sandford or Warcop) Brough provides an ideal opportunity to stock up on all those essentials (see page 54).

BROUGH

Straddling both sides of the A66 trans-Pennine road the town of Brough consists of two villages, Church Brough and Market Brough. Although there is suggested evidence that Brough existed well before, the history of this small community can only reliably be traced back to the Roman occupation of Britain.

The Romans had actually been in this country since AD 43 but had not ventured north. Their trade agreements with the north of England had served them well and in Queen Cartamandau they had a reliable ally. It was only when civil war raged throughout her Brigantian kingdom that she appealed for help from the Romans.

The Roman Army was duly despatched north, the rebels were quickly annihilated but unfortunately for Queen Cartamandau so were the whole of the royal family. If, and it seems likely, there was a settlement here, the people of Brough would have been the first Cumbrians to feast their eyes on the sight of the fearsome Roman Army as they marched across Stainmore. The Roman fort was located where the remains of the Norman Castle still stand today, without doubt a prime site, overlooking Swindale and Augill Beck's as well as having a good view of the Stainmore route.

As time passed and once again this country was governed by overseas raiders Brough became a strategic point. The 'Normans' arrived in the area in AD 1092 and promptly built a new castle on the site of the former Roman fort. Today little remains of the castle. However, there would have been considerably less had it not been for the restoration work carried out under the orders of Lady Anne Clifford in the 17th century. A visit to the remains would still provide an interesting insight into history and would be time well spent.

As with any fort or castle a community builds around it and of course Church Brough was no exception. It was not until the 14th century when a market sprung up at the crossing of Swindale Beck (the market charter was granted in 1330) that Market Brough became the dominant village.

Wherever you wander in Brough you will find evidence of a village steeped in custom. Every year until its demise in 1860 a mid-winter fire burning festival was held every Twelfth Night and on the 5th of November each year people would race down the main road with barrels of flaming tar on their heads in celebration of Guy Fawkes, on reaching the Market place discarding them onto a huge bonfire.

Although dogged by the plague in 1661 Brough continued to rise in importance and by the 18th century was a welcome stop-over point for the stage coaches that ran the two routes over Stainmore, Glasgow to London and Lancaster to Newcastle. At the time there were no fewer than seventeen pubs and inns in Brough and the 'town' would have remained an important 'staging post' but for a major blunder by the Parish Council and local landowners.

In 1856 representatives of the Darlington and Stockton Railway visited Brough to assess the possibilities of extending the line from Barnard Castle to Brough. Such was the opposition to this plan they revised their route and took the line to Kirkby Stephen.

Brough was deserted.

The clock tower which stands proudly in the centre of Market Brough was erected in 1911 and careful inspection reveals that the top portion of it is the original Market Cross. The tower itself stands over a site which was once the end of a pilgrimage for many travellers, 'St.Mary's Well'. Brough has long been associated with travel. For many years as a young boy I can vividly remember the coach stopping here as we made the long haul from Newcastle to Blackpool for the obligatory two weeks annual holiday.

FACILITIES IN BROUGH

As you would expect with a community of this size Brough provides everything the weary traveller could need. There are a number of pubs which supply a consistent stream of good quality meals and lashings of good ale. Although the shops are not as dominant as you may expect there are facilities to stock up on all supplies, something which needs to be considered as the next stretch to Middleton In Teesdale provides little in the way of facilities. B&B accommodation is available but limited so advance booking is definitely recommended. Unfortunately there is no camp site, but an enquiry at the Tourist Information Office which is situated in the mini-supermarket on the main street will probably reveal a site where your tent can be pitched for the night. Your visit to Brough can be enhanced by a publication available from the Tourist Information Centre entitled *Brough - exploring its History;* this informative leaflet gives a much more in-depth look into the trials and tribulations of this Cumbrian community.

The Clock Tower, Brough

HANDY HINTS

Not a pleasant subject to talk about but one that has affected each and every one of us from time to time, bodily functions have a tendency to require attention at the most inopportune moments and you can almost guarantee that you are miles from the nearest loo.

As a backpacker who relies on the stream water nature so kindly provides I take great exception to finding some mindless person adding to the water levels as he relieves himself oblivious to the fact that I am 100 yards downstream collecting water for a brew.

There are two ways to deal with this problem. For the perfectionist you can carry an old water bottle for urine and a plastic bag for your discarded faeces. No way, I hear you cry.

Using a knife cut a 12 inch square in the earth, lift the turf and then deepen the hole. Once relieved fill the hole and replace the square of turf. Easy and no inconvenience to others. Always carry a toilet roll in your rucksack and make sure it is kept in a waterproof bag.

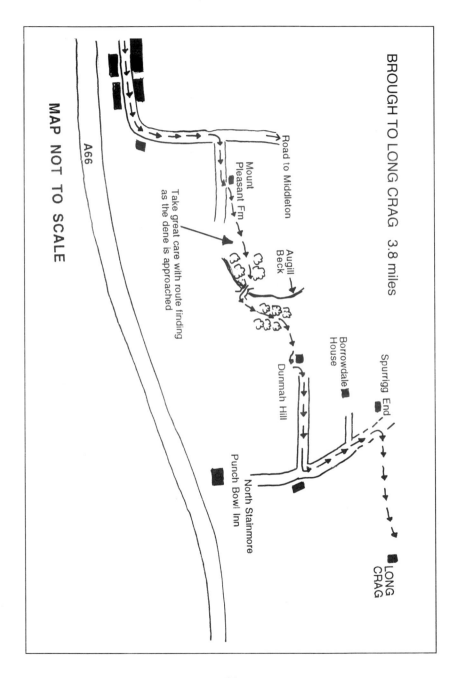

BROUGH TO LONG CRAG 3.8 miles

MAP NOT TO SCALE

A66

Road to Middleton

Mount
Pleasant Fm

Take great care with route finding
as the dene is approached

Augill
Beck

Borrowdale
House

Dunnah Hill

Spurrigg End

North Stainmore
Punch Bowl Inn

LONG
CRAG

BROUGH TO LONG CRAG FARM

3.8 miles / 6.1 Km

For almost the first sixty miles of this trek wayfinding has been relatively easy, now for the first time, as the walk enters the forbidding Pennines a knowledge of map and compass work becomes essential.

During the coming days much of the walk passes over barren moorland where 'footpaths' are luxuries that are marked on maps but are almost indistinguishable on the ground. For the experienced hiker the prospect of having to pit your wits against the landscape will be an exciting challenge but for the less experienced walker the prospects are not quite so enthralling. As the way ahead is so challenging I have devised alternative routes. Should you have any doubts whatsoever about your map reading and compass proficiency then I implore you to take the alternatives. These routes do not detract at all from the amazing scenery you are about to encounter. Whilst they do involve an amount of road walking they provide a much safer route.

IN BAD WEATHER CONDITIONS IT IS ADVISABLE THAT ALL HIKERS TAKE THE ALTERNATIVE ROUTES

Having turned right at the clock tower in the centre of Brough follow the main road through this small Pennine town. At the top of the hill the road bends round to the left. Continue to follow this out of town and proceed along this road until a fork in the road is reached. Directly ahead is the road to Middleton in Teesdale. At this point turn right and follow this quiet back road for a few hundred yards. At the brow of the hill a derelict farmhouse (Mount Pleasant) is found on the left. Turn left onto the track at the signpost which reads 'Public footpath - Dunmah Hill' and pass in front of the buildings and round to the left where a marker directs you diagonally right across the field to reach a stile. Proceed directly across the next field to another stile in the wall, once over continue straight ahead, ignoring a faint trail to your left. Ahead can be seen an old barn. Maintain your line and cross two more stiles before a gate is finally reached. Go through and head for the large wooden stile which can be seen ahead.

Once you have safely negotiated this bear slightly diagonally left to reach a crest. Take care in way finding, look to your left and in the bottom of the ravine can be seen the track. Carefully make your way down the ravine and onto this track. Very soon the footbridge is crossed and the path followed to the left. From this point way markers point the way but care is needed to ensure each one is seen. This path soon swings right and begins a short climb up through the forest.

At the first summit continue straight ahead where soon a much wider track is followed up the energy sapping climb to reach a stile opposite the farm buildings. Cross and bear right around the edge of the pasture to reach a gate at the rear of the farmhouse. Go through and onto the tarmac road. Continue along this road ignoring all footpath signs, to finally reach a junction in the road. To the right can be seen the welcoming sight of the Punch Bowl Inn at North Stainmore. Unfortunately our route now turns left.

Proceed along this road. To the right can be seen the farm at Dunmah Crag and soon to the left can be seen another farm, Borrowdale Beck. As the road reaches two gates, to the left is 'Spurring End', take the gate to the right and onto the bridleway. This continues to rise and arrives at another gate. Go through this gate and past the farmhouse on your right, which is 'Long Crag'.

FACILITIES ON THIS SECTION

The small Pennine town of Brough has a plentiful sprinkling of shops and it is advised that, as the next port of call is Middleton in Teesdale which is fifteen and a half miles away, packed lunches and drinks are purchased here.

Please note that today the walk enters the hostile Pennine areas. Route finding is not easy and the weather conditions can change extremely quickly. Please check all safety equipment and First Aid kits before venturing out.

The Bainbridge Memorial, Middleton in Teesdale

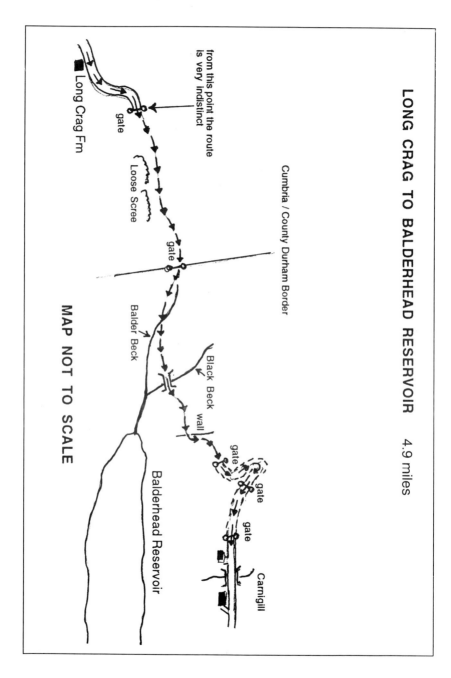

LONG CRAG TO BALDERHEAD RESERVOIR   4.9 miles

MAP NOT TO SCALE

from this point the route
is very indistinct

Long Crag Fm

gate

Loose Scree

Cumbria / County Durham Border

gate

Balder Beck

Black Beck

wall

gate

gate

gate

Carrigill

Balderhead Reservoir

60

LONG CRAG TO BALDERHEAD RESERVOIR

4.9 miles / 7.9 Km

From Long Crag Farm the track continues to wind its cheery way up the hillside until a gate is finally reached and marks the beginning of open moorland.

From this point please take great care as way-finding is difficult to say the least. Go through the gate and continue straight ahead along the 'path' which can be seen slightly to the left. As the path disintegrates a wilderness of bogs and heather lead across the open moor. On the hillside to your right can be seen some loose scree. By keeping parallel to this scree the correct line is being followed. In the distance can be seen the trig point at Great Dodd.

After a torturous walk across the moor a fence is finally reached. This marks the county boundary. As you pass through the gate let me welcome you to my home county, the spectacular County Durham. By continuing straight ahead a stream is soon found to your left. This is Balder Beck. Follow the line of this stream, crossing it at the stepping stones. At this point the way becomes a little more clear. Keep Balder Beck to your right. Soon the route crosses a stream and continues to undulate until a junction of the two streams is met at the bridge. Cross the bridge and proceed up the short but stiff little climb. Still with the beck parallel on your right a gap in the wall is reached. At this point turn sharply left, go for approximately eighty yards and turn right onto the track, once again travelling parallel to Balder Beck.

In the distance can be seen Balderhead reservoir, and the temptation to head for the track which can be seen nestling to the right should be avoided. Instead continue straight ahead to join a track which leads to a gate and onto the farm track. Proceed along this track which sweeps around the culvert to another gate. Go through and continue along the track which reaches the tarmac road at another gate. Continue straight ahead to arrive at a farm house on your right which is Balder Head.

FACILITIES ON THIS SECTION

As previously stated there are no facilities along this section.

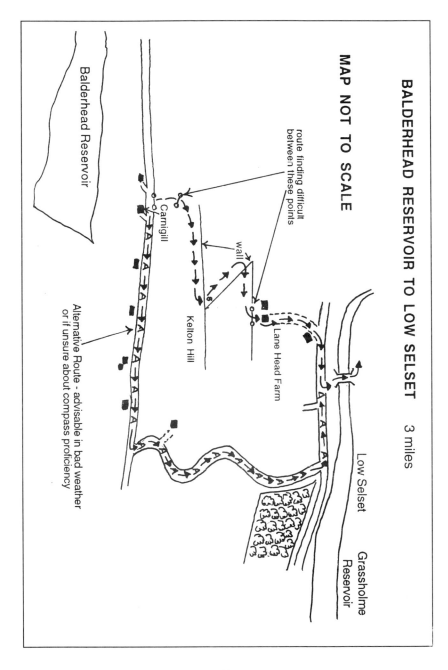

BALDERHEAD RESERVOIR TO LOW SELSET   3 miles

MAP NOT TO SCALE

route finding difficult between these points

Balderhead Reservoir

Carrigill

wall

Kelton Hill

Lane Head Farm

Alternative Route - advisable in bad weather or if unsure about compass proficiency

Low Selset

Grassholme Reservoir

BALDERHEAD RESERVOIR TO LOW SELSET

3 miles / 4.8 Km

After passing the first house on the right at Balderhead continue for a short distance up the road and across the stone bridge. Take the next turning on the left (not signposted) through the gate. Continue alongside the fence up the field to the gate at the top. At this point the path is indistinguishable; however, if you continue in a straight line you will eventually arrive at a wall which stretches all the way up Kelton Hill.

Follow the line of the wall towards the hill. Look for a wall coming up from the valley which meets the wall you are following. Just past this 'meeting' look for a hidden stile in the wall and cross over. Bear gently right to the wall where another stile is found in the bottom corner of the pasture. Cross this stile and proceed to the gate in the wall below. Walk on to the next gate and turn right through the confines of the farm buildings (Lane Head) to join the track. Follow this track all the way to the road and turn right. After only a few yards a path to the left is taken down the embankment and across the footbridge over the edge of Selset Reservoir.

Alternative route from Balderhead to Selset Reservoir

Continue along the road from Balder Head for approximately two miles, passing the farms at Foul Syke, Sleetburn and Blind Beck (all on the right). Once past Blind Beck take the next turning on the left. The quiet back road bends left and then right. Go past the access track to Hill Gill and take the next turning on the left. This leads down the side of the copse to a junction with the road. Turn left and follow the road. As the access track to Hunter House is passed take the footpath to your right which leads down and across the bridge on the edge of Selset Reservoir.

FACILITIES ON THIS SECTION

None whatsoever.

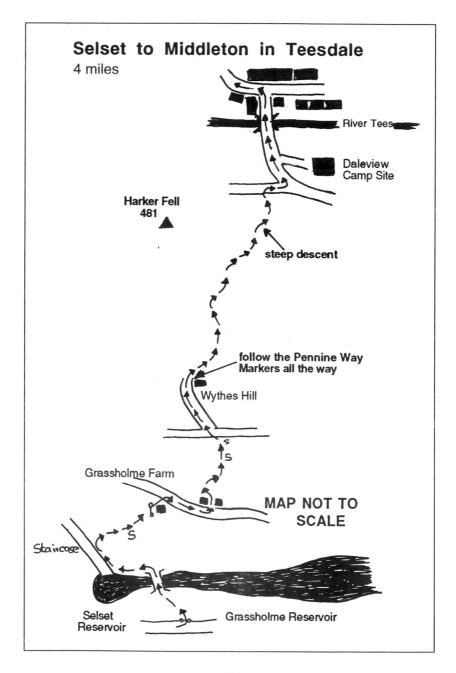

Selset to Middleton in Teesdale

4 miles

River Tees

Daleview
Camp Site

Harker Fell
481

steep descent

follow the Pennine Way
Markers all the way

Wythes Hill

S
S

Grassholme Farm

MAP NOT TO
SCALE

S

Staircase

Selset
Reservoir

Grassholme Reservoir

SELSET TO MIDDLETON IN TEESDALE

4 miles / 6.4 Km

The route now bends left and follows along the side of the reservoir for a short distance, crosses the fanciful stile (ignoring the one on your right) and begins to rise alongside the overflow staircase. Approximately half way up this climb turn sharply right which leads to the stile. Cross and bear diagonally left uphill to the gate in the electrified fence next to the farm house at Low Selset. Turn left and go through the yard and gate, continue down the fence next to the farm house at Low Selset. On reaching the road turn right. Walk along this road until arriving at the entrance to Grassholme farm on the left, at which point you will see a sign, 'Pennine Way', which is obviously some ancient walk nobody has ever heard of. Turn left and go through the yard and gate, continue down the fence next to the farm house at Low Selset. On reaching the road turn right. Continue down the pasture and turn left up the field to the stile in the wall.

The way ahead is self evident and culminates at the stile where the road is met. Continue straight ahead up this road (Wythes Hill). Pass the farmhouse and a cottage to a gateway, ignore the gate and follow the path to the right. The markers for the Pennine Way are quite prominent and provide easy way finding all the way to Middleton in Teesdale. This undulating path proceeds through a succession of gates and as the crest is finally and no doubt thankfully reached the village of Middleton can be seen in the distance below. Maintain your route following the Pennine Way and the never ending descent into this extremely popular tourist haven on the banks of the river Tees finally terminates at a meeting with the road. At this point turn right and immediately left to cross the bridge and into the centre of the village.

FACILITIES ON SECTION

On reaching the small Dales town Middleton in Teesdale there is a wealth of facilities available to you.

MIDDLETON IN TEESDALE

Situated at the gateway to the magnificent landscape of Upper Teesdale the exquisite stone built town of Middleton in Teesdale has become an extremely popular haunt for the weekend caravan dweller as well as the regular day trippers, and whilst this may seem a good reason to avoid such a place Middleton, seems to accommodate all visitors without interference to its tranquil lifestyle.

The town largely developed due to the heavy Lead Mining industry in this region. In fact Middleton housed the headquarters of the London Lead Company, evidence of which can be found in the square where stands a brightly painted cherubic cast iron fountain which was built by R.W. Bainbridge of Middleton House and commemorates a testimonial presented to him by the employees of the London Lead Company. The LLC was a Quaker organisation and took great pride in ensuring the welfare of their employees and their families. A school, chapel, library and solidly built cottages were all provided for the workers.

Exploring the town it comes as no surprise to find that Middleton boasts a fine Parish Church. Built in 1557 on the site of a former church it was the only church within the county of Durham that had its own detached belfry. The idea of a parson aptly named William Bell, I kid you not. The belfry housed three bells, one of which still survives today, and would be played by a local man using both hands and one of his feet.

Near to the churchyard gate is the original 13th century east window but for the more inquisitive visitor a glimpse inside the church reveals a wealth of historical interest. In the north wall of the nave can be seen some magnificent examples of mediaeval gravestones, superbly carved and depicting everything from floral crosses to mining tools. Also of interest is the font. Try counting the number of sides this unique structure bears.

This solidly built town is also the birthplace of Richard Watson. Born in 1833 he was seconded into the lead mining industry at the tender age of ten and went on to become one of the best loved poets in the north of England, his *Poems and Songs of Teesdale* expressing explicitly in local dialect the harshness of reality of life in the mines. Middleton is a welcoming town and the local community extremely hospitable.

FACILITIES IN MIDDLETON IN TEESDALE

Although only a small town Middleton does provide almost everything you could need. There are a number of shops and some well appointed pubs, most of which provide evening meals. As the route heads northwards once again over the barren moors of the Pennines, facilities are non-existent until Stanhope is reached, therefore replenishing the stocks in Middleton is a must. For backpackers the camp site on the right as you enter Middleton provides a superb stop over. With good pitches and superb meals this venue is a must.

LEAD MINING BENEATH THE NORTHERN PENNINES

As someone who was born and bred in the North East of England, I have always had a deep-rooted respect for the coal mining communities that once prospered here. The hardships they endured both in the dangerous nature of their work and their struggle against oppression are well documented.

As the walk now enters the Northern Pennines the remains of old mine workings start to appear on the landscape. These are not the remains of coal mines but of an industry that records an even harsher lifestyle, the now almost forgotten industry of lead mining.

Almost exclusive to this part of the country the history of lead mining can be traced back centuries, in fact to mediaeval England when the all powerful Prince Bishops were granted mineral rights and pocketed one-ninth of all produce as royalties. At first the lead was simply dug out with crude tools but it was not long before 'hushing' was introduced. 'Hushing' was a method whereby a dam would be constructed and when enough water had been gathered to create a rushing head it would be released. The torrent of water would sweep down the hillside removing the loose earth to reveal the deposit of lead in the rock below.

Lead mining varies greatly from its coal counterpart; whereas a coal seam is a deposit and travels generally horizontally a lead vein is caused by a metallic intrusion penetrating vertically through the rocks. A seam can end without warning although, some of the veins run for more than a mile underground.

By the 18th century the demand for lead was growing as domestic and foreign needs escalated but it was mainly due to military requirements that the whole industry had to be overhauled. In 1776 the price of a 'bing'(21 hundredweight) had been £12, but with ammunition needed for the Napoleonic Wars the price rocketed to £40. Owners made vast fortunes overnight, new shafts were sunk, old ones repaired and miners drafted in from as far away as Cornwall and Ireland (it is hard to imagine their reactions when they first arrived at this barren wilderness). Mining was carried out by driving tunnels or 'levels' into the hillside; the entrances, many of which can still be seen today, were arched and made from local stone. Timber rail wagonways forged their way to the seam where ponies would haul the galena or lead sulphide out of the mine to the waiting gang of 'galloways'.

The 'galloways' were a hardy breed of horse and a gang normally consisted of 15-20 animals. Being sure-footed they were ideally suited for the long and arduous task of carrying the lead across the bleak moors. During the long days of the summer months countless gangs could be seen from dawn until dusk making their way to and from the smelting mills. It would not be long before the mining companies laid roads and these horses would become redundant.

By the 19th century there were in excess of 6,000 miners and their families living in this region, forging a meagre living for themselves and satisfying the insatiable demand for lead.

The life of lead miners was never easy. As well as living in continuous danger within the job, they also had to endure the rigours of life high in the Pennines. In the early days the mines were small and the communities scattered; only at the smelting mills was the populous more concentrated. Often surviving on a staple diet of rye bread the families became more and more dependent upon the smallholdings which they tended while the man worked at the mine. Here crops such as potatoes and other basic vegetables would be grown, the climate not allowing for much else.

Though life was undoubtedly hard the mining community was deeply religious. John Wesley and his preachers were frequent visitors to this region between 1752 and 1790.

At first the community would gather in each other's homes for their services but soon small chapels started to dot the landscape. Many of these chapels, survive to this day. Some of which can be seen on this route.

The great love of the miners was 'ale'. Unfortunately for them (but I should imagine pleasing for the employers) they were only paid once a month and so the drinking bouts were generally curtailed. This was until the payout from the annual account was due when mines would close for two weeks and basically all hell would break loose. Such was the reputation of the miners they were actually banned from entering the city of Newcastle and therefore headed off to the next nearest place, Blaydon.

By the 1870s the lead industry had gone into decline and it never recovered. The walk through the Northern Pennines relives this amazing period of industrial and religious history. As you walk across this beautiful yet bleak landscape it is easy to go back in time and perhaps experience a little of what it may have been like here centuries ago.

Today, lead mining is remembered in the dales at the Killhope Leadmining Centre in Weardale. This exciting museum is unfortunately well away from the actual route but it does provide a superb history learning opportunity and is well worth a visit at some time in the future.

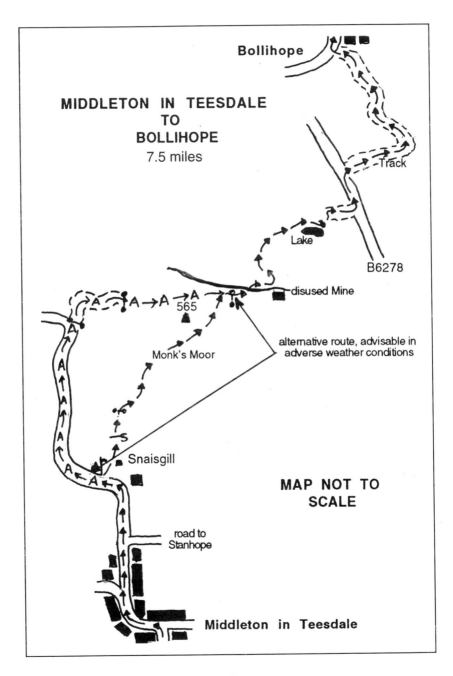

Bollihope

MIDDLETON IN TEESDALE
TO
BOLLIHOPE
7.5 miles

Track

Lake

B6278

disused Mine

A A A A
565

alternative route, advisable in
adverse weather conditions

Monk's Moor

S

Snaisgill

MAP NOT TO
SCALE

road to
Stanhope

Middleton in Teesdale

MIDDLETON IN TEESDALE TO BOLLIHOPE

7.5 miles / 12 Km

As with the previous section this route calls for a good knowledge of map and compass work. If in any doubt please follow the alternative route provided.

From the entrance to Dale View Caravan and Camping Park continue straight down the road and across the bridge. On reaching the road junction in the centre of the town turn left and then cross the road to pass the Teesdale Hotel. Continue up this road and take the minor road directly in front of you, signposted 'Stanhope 11 miles'. The road now starts a long climb passing St. Mary's Church and is followed all the way to reach another signpost which can be somewhat disheartening as it reads 'Stanhope 11 miles' (someone cannot count).

Ignore this turning on your right and proceed up the road to Snaisgill. Pass the farm on the right and soon some cottages are passed before the road swings sharply left. As soon as the bend is rounded a sign on the right reads 'Public footpath - Frosterley'. At this point a decision is needed. If you are unsure about map and compass work or the weather is at all inclement then please follow the alternative route, which does include another two miles of road and track walking but does not detract from the splendid scenery encountered on this section.

Alternative route to the disused mine workings near White Hill

Ignore the footpath sign for Frosterley and continue to follow the quiet back road. As the road makes a sweeping curve to the right Hudeshope Beck can be seen in the valley below. Follow this access road all the way until a gate is reached. Go through and as the access road now turns sharply left continue straight ahead up the old mine track.

Soon the track begins the long haul as it sweeps right. Half way up the climb take the track that leads off to the right which in turn leads to a gate. Go through the gate and continue to follow the track which soon reverts to a fainter footpath but is still relatively easy to follow. Once over the summit the path heads steeply downhill and wayfinding becomes a little more difficult. However, as long as you continue to head for the former mine workings in the valley below you are on course.

Half way down the descent a stile is crossed before the valley bottom is reached beside Great Egglestone Beck. Turn right through the gate and proceed alongside the stream, soon crossing at the stepping stones. As a junction of tracks is met the bridge can be seen to your right. Ignore this and the very sharp turning on your immediate left which basically leads back the way you came, instead taking the second turning on the left which leads up another well defined track.

For more experienced walkers, on reaching the 'Frosterley' footpath sign go through the gate and bear immediately left through another gate. This then climbs the field to another gate in the middle of the wall. Continue the climb to reach another gate at the corner of the wall. From this point the route starts to bear right away from the wall and continues along that line across the open moor to arrive at a shooting house. This is passed on the right side still maintaining the same bearing.

Soon the old mine workings are seen in the valley below. Start the descent which in turn leads to the derelict buildings at the mine. Cross Great Egglestone Beck at the concrete bridge and proceed straight ahead, ignoring the two turnings on your left (at this point the alternative route rejoins the L21 route).

Once again a pleasant climb begins and as the track starts to disintegrate a gate is reached where a derelict building can be seen to your right. Follow the path slightly to the left and continue the climb. As the path finally fades into obscurity great care is needed in locating the route. Cross the stream and turn right on to a very faint path which can just be made out in the heather to a much wider track and a gate. Once through proceed once again uphill to meet the road. On reaching the B6278 turn left and follow the road over the crest past the Weardale 'border' and as the road starts to drop down the hill an access track is found on the right. Turn right onto this track and it will be pleasing to know that after the rigours of way finding across the moor you can now relax and enjoy the scenery as the track slowly bears left and winds its way down to the tiny hamlet at Bollihope

FACILITIES ON THIS SECTION

None whatsoever after leaving Middleton in Teesdale. There is nothing available until Stanhope or Wolsingham.

HANDY HINTS

Today, 'walking poles' are becoming a more and more frequent sight on the hills of this country. In the past two years I have been carrying out tests on these aids and have found them to be extremely beneficial (especially for us old timers). Using two of these poles both ascending and descending becomes much easier and can save up to 40% of energy expended.

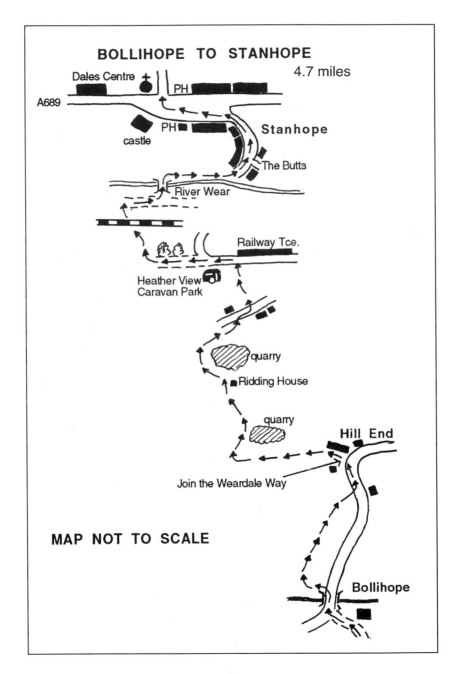

BOLLIHOPE TO STANHOPE

4.7 miles

Dales Centre

A689

PH

PH
castle

Stanhope

The Butts

River Wear

Railway Tce.

Heather View
Caravan Park

quarry

Ridding House

quarry

Hill End

Join the Weardale Way

MAP NOT TO SCALE

Bollihope

BOLLIHOPE TO STANHOPE

4.7 miles / 7.6 Km

Once the track culminates at the road in Bollihope turn right and cross the open bridge across Bollihope Burn. Turn immediately left along the river bank for approximately thirty yards and then turn sharply right up the steep incline. As the first ridge is reached a way marker (remember them?) is found.

Continue to climb and very soon a more defined track is found. Turn right and keeping parallel with the road keep climbing all the way to rejoin the road opposite the cottage at the brow of the hill. Follow the road until just prior to the cattle grid in Hill End, as the signpost for 'The Weardale Way' is found turn left along this grassy track.

'The Weardale Way' is an ancient footpath which follows the course of the River Wear from its source high in the Pennines to its spill into the North Sea at Sunderland. Until 1996 this walk had fallen into oblivion but with the co-operation of Durham County Council yours truly totally re-designed it and is now an extremely popular walk, also the subject of my second book.

The crest is finally reached as the wall to the right ends. The superb view across the whole of Weardale certainly makes the long haul worthwhile. There now follows another open moorland walk, following the line of the wall on the right and ignoring all other trails. Eventually the wall comes to an end at a junction with the wall coming down from the moor. Turn right and cross the stile. With the wall now on your left continue down to the gate at the bottom. As the route begins to rise turn left through a gate and head for the gate in the wall to the right. This leads to the derelict remains of Ridding House. Go through the gate and turn left along the track to another gate. Walk diagonally to the right to join the fence above the quarry.

Follow this track straight ahead to a hole in the wall, go through and follow the track in a loop to cross the small burn at the stepping stones. Proceed uphill past the fenced off shake hole and through the gate on the left. The route follows the fence to its conclusion where a brick outhouse can be seen to the left.

Continue straight ahead to join the track and turn left down the gravelled road, passing between the first buildings to a stone stile on the left. Cross straight over to another stile after which head diagonally across the field towards the row of houses which can be seen below. Cross the stile and turn left along this quiet back road.

Soon the entrance to Heather View Caravan Park is found. Proceed straight through the site to a stile at the end. Now alongside the River Wear a short woodland walk ensues and arrives at a stile. Cross and after another fifty yards the route bends sharply left and leads to two stiles crossing the now disused railway line. Once over proceed along the well defined path towards Unthank Mill and cross the footbridge over the river. Turn right and follow the riverside path. As the houses are reached a road leads gently uphill to arrive in the centre of Stanhope.

FACILITIES IN STANHOPE AND WOLSINGHAM

Although neither can be regarded as 'towns', both Stanhope and Wolsingham offer good facilities for the visitor. Backpackers are limited as to their choice of overnight stay. Stanhope offers the only facilities in the area. For more information ask at The Dales Centre.

As well as the pleasing sight of many ale houses they both have small 'supermarkets' and a host of other shops. I would strongly advise stocking up well at either of these places as facilities between here and Allendale (another 25 miles along the route) can be somewhat hit and miss.

The Mill Race, Wolsingham

St. Thomas Church, Stanhope

STANHOPE

Standing proud in the shadow of the Northern Pennines Stanhope was once at the very heart of life in this working dale. Today this sleepy little town with its battle torn history is only disturbed by the constant thunder of cement laden juggernauts as they rush their cargo to and from the nearby works at Eastgate. Whilst the works do provide valuable employment for people in the region it is still a shame that the railway once used for the transportation of cement stands idle and decaying.

The history of Stanhope can be traced back many centuries, the name itself being a direct translation from the Celtic language, meaning 'stony valley'. The centre of the town is dominated by St.Thomas' church which was built circa AD 1200, although the north and south aisles were added as late as the 19th century. Even before entering the church history engulfs you. Outside the gates stands the old cross erected when Stanhope was granted a market charter in 1421, a charter held until late in the 19th century. The church wall allows the visitor to glimpse the fossilised tree unearthed on moorland near Edmundbyers and believed to be more than 250 million years old.

As the grounds are entered a large tombstone to the left denotes the final resting place of the Bainbridge family, famous for their Department stores, which are still alive today as part of the John Lewis Partnership. Further to the left a 13th century stone coffin stands open and is flanked by other stones manufactured from locally quarried 'Frosterley Marble'.

On entering the church one cannot help feeling a little humbled as two heads peer inquisitively down from their perch in the chancel arch. Directly ahead the north wall boasts two black oak plaques depicting Christ with St. Peter and Adam and Eve, a superb example of the craftsmanship of the Flemish carvers who created them. The stained glass windows are a joy to behold especially the west window which dates back to the 14th century.

On the opposite side of the road stands Stanhope 'Castle', a title barely deserved when you consider it was only built in 1798 as a gentleman's retreat and has never been a fortified stronghold. In 1875 the 'castle' was enlarged to cater for the ever growing numbers of people taking up the 'sport' of grouse shooting. Since that time the building has been used as a school and today is sub-divided into private flats.

Keepers employed by the Bishop of Durham had captured a gang of local lead miners poaching and incarcerated them in one of the rooms whilst awaiting transport to Durham jail. When their colleagues heard where they were being held they attacked the Inn, releasing their compatriots and leaving the keepers with a severe beating. No one was ever brought to justice for this savage behaviour; only the curdled blood stains left testament to 'the battle of Stanhope'.

Opposite stands the Pack Horse Inn, once a staging post for the Rob Roy Stagecoach, whilst nearby are 'The Butts', as the name implies, an area which was frequently used by archers in the days of the longbow. Stanhope also boasts two other pubs, the Queen's Head and, to the west of the town, the Grey Bull.

Travelling a little further west stands Stanhope Hall. Built in mediaeval times this somewhat unattractive building also served as a hunting lodge for the Prince Bishops of Durham. Probably best described as a prime example of mediaeval/Elizabethan/Jacobean architecture its distinct lack of windows dates back to when buildings taxes were levied on the number of windows each building had.

The first recorded keepers of the Hall were the Featherstonhaugh family in AD 1135 during the reign of King Stephen. Many famous people throughout history have stayed here, Bishop Pudsey, Richard I's regent for Northern England and Edward, the Black Prince, in 1327 to name but two. The hall remained in the custodial hands of the Featherstonhaughs until 1704 when Colonel Featherstonhaugh was killed at the battle of Blenheim. For a short period the Bainbridges resided here but in 1798 it became the property of Cuthbert Rippon MP, as did much of Stanhope. Today the property serves as a hotel and restaurant and is an historic setting for a well earned cuppa.

Personally, I like Stanhope and especially the people. They are living and working in one of the last working dales left in this country and go about their business accordingly, whilst they provide a warm welcome to the visitor they do so without being intrusive. Stanhope also boasts a fine 'Dales Centre' where the Tourist Information Office is the most helpful I have found to date. A wealth of informative literature is available to enhance your visit.

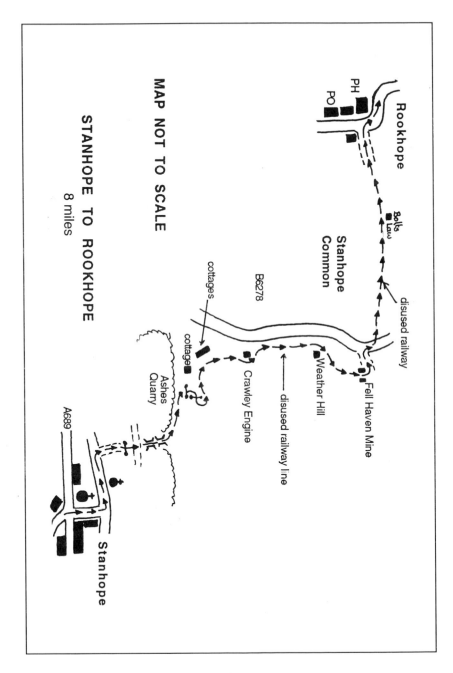

MAP NOT TO SCALE

STANHOPE TO ROOKHOPE

8 miles

Rookhope

PH

PO

Bolts
Law

Stanhope
Common

disused railway

B6278

cottages

cottage

Ashes
Quarry

Crawley Engine

Weather Hill

disused railway line

Fell Haven Mine

A689

Stanhope

STANHOPE TO ROOKHOPE

8 miles / 12.9 Km

From the centre of Stanhope cross the road and between St. Thomas' Church and the Bonny Moor Hen public house a lane leads up Church Lane. On reaching the junction at the top turn left and follow the road until just past the Methodist Church. At this point a well hidden enclosed footpath leads off to the right and begins to ascend the hill. Soon a gate is passed through and the path arrives at a junction.

Continue straight ahead and carefully cross the two footbridges which lead over Ashes Quarry. This leads up to a stile. Cross and follow the line of the fence, which should be to your left, around the top side of the quarry. As the gentle climb continues look to the right and prior to the cottage a gate can be seen. Go through this gate and turn immediately right again through the other gate which is only a matter of feet away. Once through turn left and follow the fairly distinct path all the way to the summit.

By following this trail a wall appears on the left. At this point the route begins to bear right and follows around the ridge, behind the outbuildings of what was once the Crawley Engine House. At the end of the wall a track is met; turn left and follow the indistinct trail around to the right to join the now disused railway line. Looking directly ahead on the skyline the former Weather Hill Engine House can be seen. The line is followed all the way to reach this interesting relic of the Lead Mining Industry where, incidentally, some of the old hauling machinery still exists.

Once at Weather Hill go past the buildings and the path swings gently to the right for a short period before once again running parallel with the road and following the old line all the way to the now derelict Fell Haven Mine which can be seen in the distance. Pass between the buildings and turn left along the access track passing a cottage on the left before the track eventually meets the B6278.

At this point turn right and follow the road for only a few yards before turning left onto the distinct footpath. This footpath is in fact the old railway line across Stanhope Common and now acts as part of the C2C cycle route. There now follows a splendid walk across the moor (in good weather) with views right across the northern Pennines. After a little more than a mile an access track is reached; cross straight over and continue to follow the trail which starts to swing gently left and eventually arrives at the old engine house at Bolt's Law, which marks the summit. Still following the line of the old railway the route now drops sharply, and once through a gate an access track leads all the way into the tiny village of Rookhope, where the road is met.

FACILITIES ON THIS SECTION

After leaving Stanhope there is nothing at all until Rookhope is reached where a small shop/Post Office serves the tiny community.

The Rookhope Inn

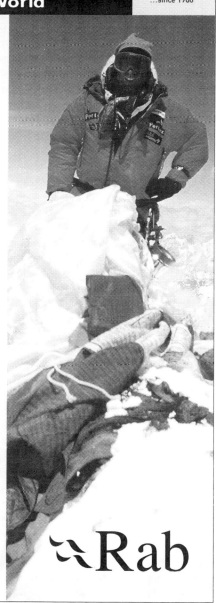

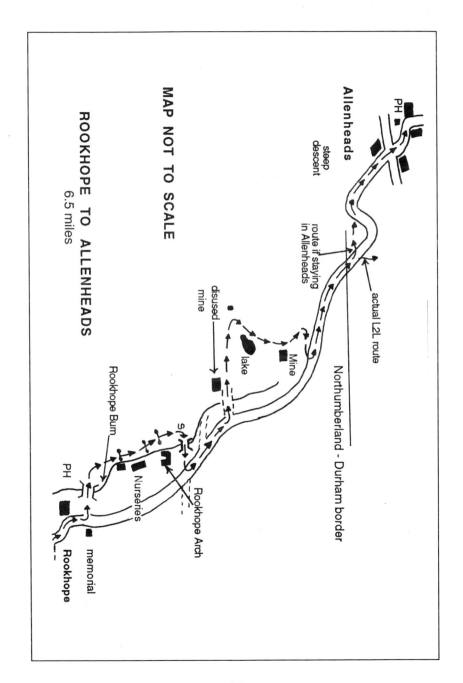

MAP NOT TO SCALE

ROOKHOPE TO ALLENHEADS
6.5 miles

Allenheads

PH

steep
descent

route if staying
in Allenheads

actual L2L route

Northumberland - Durham border

disused
mine

lake

Mine

Rookhope Burn

PH

Nurseries

Rookhope Arch

memorial

Rookhope

ROOKHOPE TO ALLENHEADS

6.5 miles / 10.5 Km

On reaching the road turn right and follow it past the Rookhope Inn and around to the right across the bridge. When opposite the war memorial turn sharply left down a track which bends to the right and crosses a bridge. As the bridge is crossed a sign can be seen saying 'Rookhope Trails'; ignore this and continue directly ahead towards the sheds. Pass them on the right side and continue up the rise. As more sign posts are reached turn right and follow the indistinct path through the industrial debris.

Way finding is hazardous but soon a wall is reached where the path crosses a tiny stream and drops sharply to a stile in the fence ahead. Cross the stile and continue straight ahead. Whilst the path is not distinct, keeping Rookhope Burn to your right ensures the correct route is being followed. As a house is reached pass behind the shed and cross the stile. The path now joins the track and passes to the left of the Garden Nursery buildings.

Another stile is crossed and the way ahead becomes more evident. Whilst continuing along this track the remains of the 'Rookhope Arch' can be seen ahead. Pass through two gates and as a stile is reached with the farm buildings at Lintzgarth on the left, cross and turn right, crossing the small footbridge. This leads up to the road where another stile is crossed before turning left along the road. There now follows a road walk of a mile and a half, and as you are walking this stretch you will no doubt be aware of what looks like a footpath just to the left of the fence. Unfortunately this is not the case and is private land.

Still on the road and still climbing pass the entrance to Wolf Cleugh Farm continue for another half mile where a track is found to the left. Go through the gate and down the track which leads to the old mine buildings in the bottom. Cross the bridge passing the buildings which should be to the left and follow the track which starts to snake its way up the hill. A junction of tracks is soon met; turn right and after 50 yards bear left, still climbing and heading towards the corrugated building which can be seen ahead. Approximately 100 yards before reaching that building take the track which turns right past the old reservoir.

This easy-to-follow track is now followed all the way to the mine ahead (still operating at the time of writing). As the mine is finally passed the track culminates at a gate. Go through, and very soon another track is met. At this point turn left and proceed to another set of buildings which are soon encountered. Continue past the buildings through the stockyard and as the yard ends a track leads sharply off to the right. Climb this track, through the gate and back onto the road. After turning left another road walk ensues. This never-ending climb continues and is only highlighted by the crossing of the Durham/ Northumbria border.

Once the brow of the climb has been reached it is only a short walk before a decision needs to be made. If you are staying overnight in Allenheads, which will be an experience you will never forget (see below), take the footpath off to the left which leads down hill and across the stile. Once over head diagonally left across the pasture to another stile which leads back onto the road. Turn left and follow the road all the way into Allenheads itself. Be warned: if you are staying in Allenheads overnight you will have the unenviable task of retracing your steps back up this sizeable climb to where you originally left the road. If you are not staying in Allenheads then continue a little further down the road to find a sign on the right reading 'Public Footpath - Byerhope Bank 2'. At this point turn right and follow the well defined footpath.

ALLENHEADS

As the picturesque village is first glimpsed it is hard to imagine that this tiny community once produced more than one seventh of all lead mined in this country. Before the advent of the mining industry the area was preserved as a hunting ground which resulted in little population and just a sprinkling of farms. It was only when mining started that the village sprang to life and began to prosper.

During the nineteenth century as the 'lead rush' gathered momentum more than two thousand men, women and children were employed in the industry within the Allenheads area. With the mines long since gone the village, reputed to be the highest in England, has a population of nearer two hundred and survives mainly owing to the fabulous grouse shooting moors which surround it, sustaining the local economy. Tourism also plays a significant part in the village. There are a number of bunkhouse facilities for overnight accommodation and a visit to the Hemmel Coffee Shop is a must for anyone wishing to sample home cooked fare at its very best.

What makes Allenheads so special is the Allenheads Inn, situated in the heart of the village. It was built in 1770 for Sir Thomas Wentworth, Baron of Bretton and originally served as a temperance hotel.

Over the past few years it has been transformed into a Pub which has become a Mecca for visitors from all over the world. With more than five thousand items of nostalgia hanging from the ceilings, adorning the walls and almost obliterating the bar the place is veritable feast of interest and fun. The pub also provides splendid accommodation, with eight beautifully appointed bedrooms and meals that lack nothing in either quality or quantity.

The Allenheads Inn

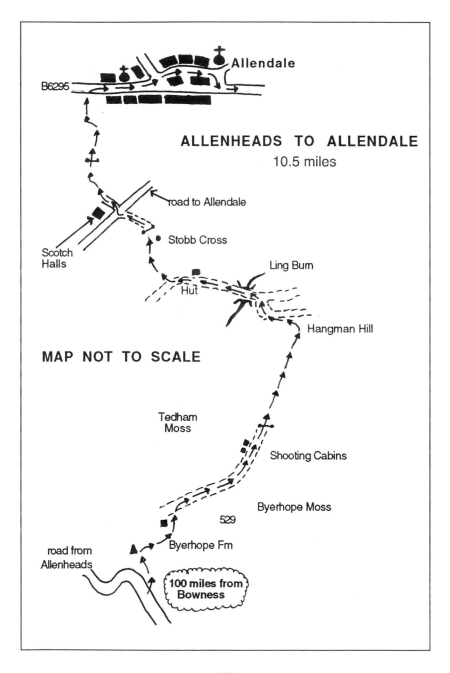

Allendale

B6295

ALLENHEADS TO ALLENDALE
10.5 miles

road to Allendale

Stobb Cross

Scotch
Halls

Ling Burn

Hut

Hangman Hill

MAP NOT TO SCALE

Tedham
Moss

Shooting Cabins

Byerhope Moss

529

road from
Allenheads

Byerhope Fm

**100 miles from
Bowness**

ALLENHEADS TO ALLENDALE TOWN

10.5 miles / 16.9 Km

If you have stayed overnight in Allenheads you now have the opportunity to wear off a large breakfast and retrace your steps back to the top of the hill overlooking the village. On reaching the road turn left and on the right hand side of the road is the signpost for Byerhope Bank. Turn along this pathway, through the gate and keep heading towards the cairn at the summit, an idyllic spot to rest after the hard climb where Allenheads can be seen in the valley below nestling under the shelter of Allendale Common. The view across the wide expanse of open moorland is really special and is a joy to behold.

From the cairn the path starts to swing right. Easy to follow, it allows ample time to milk every moment of these panoramic views. As the path starts to descend it passes an unoccupied farm building and proceeds past Byerhope Farm which is to the left. As the track ends at a junction turn right and continue the climb up this equally well defined track.

As the trig point is passed the track levels out and provides a pleasant stroll across the open moor. By continuing to follow the track two shooting huts are eventually reached. Keep to the track until the track finally ends at a gate. From this point the route is along a bridleway and is therefore not quite as well defined; however with due care route finding should not be a problem as the way continues to cross the moor. As a copse of trees is seen over to your right the route once again starts to rise gently to a gate in a fence approaching the summit. Go through the gate and continue straight ahead.

Now descending Pikeley Rigg, follow the line of the fence which should be to your left until a gate is reached approximately two thirds of the way down. Go through this gate and bear gently right, once again following a reasonably trodden pathway. To the right is the interestingly named 'Hangman Hill'. The route drops into a shallow dip before gently rising once again to arrive at a cross-roads of bridleways. At this point turn left and proceed along the length of this track until another junction is reached. Turn left, crossing the rickety bridge and follow the trail up the hill to a corrugated hut near the top of the climb.

Continue past this hut and look ahead where another hut can be seen. Just prior to reaching it and without crossing the bridge turn right onto the bridleway. A short climb ensues and soon starts to run parallel with a wall on your right. Eventually this path drops sharply into a gulley and proceeds straight up the short but demanding climb directly ahead. Still with the wall to your right 'Stobb Cross' can be seen on the skyline. Soon after the wall is left as it veers sharply away to the right, a junction of bridleways is reached.

Continue straight ahead signposted 'Public Bridleway - Allendale Town 2'. This crosses the moor and arrives at a gate. Go through the gate and proceed down the track to its conclusion where it meets the road. Turn right and then first left 'Public Footpath - Allendale 1', which leads past Scotch Hall Farm and bears right where a stile is found in the wall on the left. Go across this small pasture to another stile which is clearly marked.

Once over this the route follows directly across the field where a gate and stile can be seen in the far corner. Cross the stile and pass in front of the house (Finney Hill). To the right of the trees at the corner of the wall another stile is then crossed. Continue directly across the field with a wall to your left. Skirting the edge of the copse more stiles are crossed until finally you reach the access track for the farm house. Cross straight over and over the stile opposite, then bear left to a stile in the trees. Go over and turn sharply right and begin the horrific descent down to meet the main road. Once over the stile turn right and follow the road all the way for the short walk into the centre of Allendale.

FACILITIES ON THIS SECTION

As well as the amazing Inn the tiny hamlet of Allenheads also has a small shop and Post Office. The Hemel Coffee Shop can provide all the sustenance you need for the walk across the fells to Allendale.

ALLENDALE

The old Northumbrian town of Allendale, originally known as Allenton when first granted its charter by Edward I, was once at the heart of the Lead Mining industry so prominent within this region. As the industry slipped into terminal decline so did the population. At the turn of the twentieth century more than five thousand people lived and worked in the area; today less than two thousand remain.

But Allendale has survived. Like so many other communities faced with a similar problem it has diversified and today attracts visitors from all over the world. Not only does the area offer superb open fell walking country but it is famous for its annual 'Baal Fire'. Held each New Year's Eve this ceremony dates back to pagan times and is often linked, whether correctly or not, with the Norse invasion of northern England.

The ceremony itself involves forty local men (Guisers) blackening their faces and dressing in peculiar costume. At 11.30 p.m. they gather and, to the accompaniment of the local band playing 'Wi a hundred pipers', parade around the village with barrels of flaming tar (baals or barls) on their heads. Just prior to the sounding of midnight these baals are tossed onto a specially prepared bonfire in the square. As the church rings in the new year the guisers begin their task of 'first footing' at houses in the immediate vicinity.

Allendale's other claim to fame is that it boasts to be the exact geographical centre of Great Britain. On the outside wall of St. Cuthbert's Church a sundial can be seen commemorating this fact. The church itself was only built in 1873, but a house of worship has stood here since AD 1174 when the 'Our Lady of Allendale' was given to the Prior of Hexham. A new church was built in the fourteenth century and further buildings erected in 1807. How did the church become St. Cuthbert's? Well, your guess is as good as anyone else's, as no-one rightly knows.

As previously mentioned the area boasts some wonderful open fell walking and tourism is now playing a big part in the revival of the area. With a host of welcoming pubs and accommodation plentiful the village of Allendale would make a splendid base.

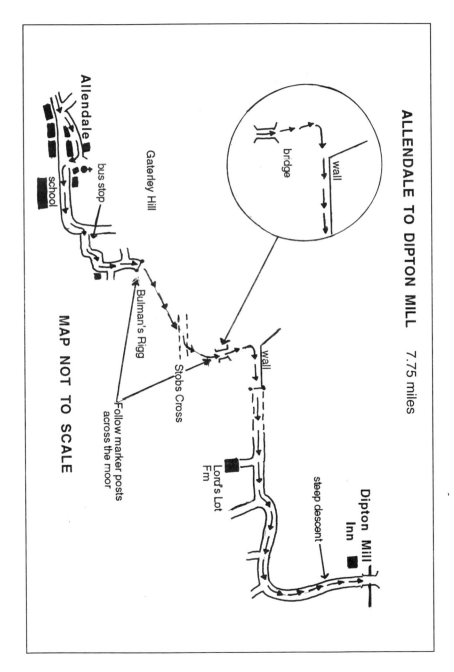

ALLENDALE TO DIPTON MILL   7.75 miles

MAP NOT TO SCALE

Allendale

bus stop

school

Gaterley Hill

Bulman's Rigg

Stobs Cross

Follow marker posts across the moor

bridge

wall

wall

Lord's Lot Fm

steep descent

Dipton Mill Inn

ALLENDALE TOWN TO DIPTON MILL

7.75 miles / 12.5 Km

From the centre of Allendale follow the road for Hexham (B6303) past the school which is to the right and soon to cross an old stone bridge as the road sweeps left. Immediately after the bend a bus stop can be seen on the right hand side of the road. Turn right up the lane next to this and begin the long ascent up this quiet back road.

Continue to follow the road, ignoring all marked footpaths. Soon the road bends sharply to the right and heads towards the barn which can be seen ahead. (As the turn is made pause and take advantage of the magnificent views back across Hexhamshire Common.) Keep to the road, ignoring the turning on the right just past the barn until, approximately 100 yards later the road bends left towards Hope Farm. At this point leave the road for the earthy track and continue straight ahead. As the crest is finally within sight a line of trees is passed, which in turn leads to the twin gates directly ahead. (In adverse weather conditions it is advisable to take a compass bearing at this point as the walk is about to proceed over open moor.)

Once through the gates head downhill along the track, which bends right and then left before beginning to climb once again. Halfway up the climb a trig point can be seen to the left; however, take the smaller path off to the right leading to 'Bulman's Rigg'. The two paths run parallel for a short while until the route veers sharply to the right, past the wooden stake. Once again we are heading into open fell country, alas for the last time on this walk.

The way ahead is carefully negotiated by following the line of guide posts across the fell, soon to reach a small footbridge across a burn. Once again continue to follow the line of posts which eventually arrives at a track. Turn right and follow this track for approximately 100 yards to a guide post on the left marked 'Public Bridleway'. Turn onto this faint path and continue to follow the line of marker posts. Ahead can be seen a copse which the route passes on the left side. At this point the posts are a little less frequent, but by maintaining a straight line a small bridge is soon reached.

Cross the bridge and please express great caution in route finding as it can be described as hazardous to say the least. Proceed up the path which is directly in front of you as you cross the bridge. As the summit is reached look for a wall on your right. At this point turn sharply right and follow the line of the wall (so that the wall is on your left) to the gate at the top. This in turn leads onto a track, soon becoming tarmac as the entrance to Lord's Lot Farm is passed. At this point a look back and you can bid a no doubt fond farewell to open country.

Choking back the tears proceed up the road passing a trig point on the right until, as the road bends sharply to the right, a gate to the left is passed through and the very faint trail followed to the gate next to the copse. The path across the fields is not easy to determine. The easiest way to ensure you are right is to look ahead, where thick clumps of trees can be seen both left and right on the skyline, and a much thinner growth can be clearly seen in the centre. Head for this gap where a gate is found.

The Square in Allendale

Go through the gate and follow the track directly ahead through a succession of gates (watch out for the Bull) until the road is finally met. To the distant left can be seen a very large white building dominating the landscape. This is the main grandstand of Hexham Racecourse, a National Hunt circuit we pass later in the day. Proceed straight ahead and follow this road all the way downhill soon becoming quite steep as it arrives in the sleepy little hamlet of Dipton Mill and the welcoming sight of the Dipton Mill Inn.

FACILITIES ON THIS SECTION

Stocks should be replenished in Allendale as there is absolutely nothing in the way of facilities until Dipton Mill is reached. Even on arriving at this hamlet there is no shop or such, but there is the very charismatic Dipton Mill Inn. Open from 12 to 2.30pm this small but welcoming hostelry supplies a wide choice of hearty and wholesome home cooked meals. The beer is quite special, brewed only a couple of miles away at the Hexhamshire Brewery. 'Shire', 'Devils Water' and 'Whapweasel' all stand up well to the test of even the most discerning palate. But beware for a hearty climb beckons.There are a number of Taxi firms in the area and the hospitality here is well worth the fare. So why not return here this evening?

HANDY HINTS

Liquid intake is essential during any hike and you must always ensure that the body is supplied with a regular supply throughout the day (not alcohol). As energy is sapped the body loses fluid at an alarming rate and if not checked will lead to severe trauma. Recognising the signs of dehydration is therefore a must. Know the 12 points .... 1. Thirst 2. Discomfort 3. Loss of appetite 4. Nausea 5. Headache 6. Dizziness 7. Speech impediment 8. Breathing irregularity 9. Inability to walk 10. Senses begin to fail 11. Inability to swallow 12. Collapse

---

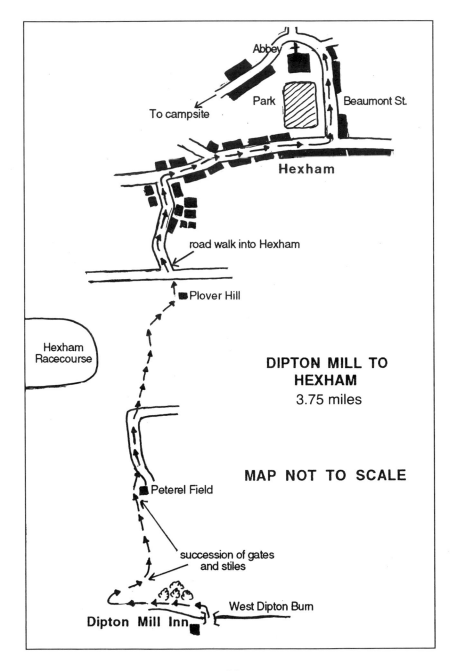

DIPTON MILL TO HEXHAM
3.75 miles

MAP NOT TO SCALE

DIPTON MILL TO HEXHAM

3.25 miles / 5.2 Km

To leave Dipton Mill cross the road bridge where a public footpath on the left is taken. This leads somewhat precariously through West Dipton Burn where way finding can be difficult. Basically stay parallel with the river, approximately half way up the embankment, and the correct line is being followed. This woodland walk passes over a couple of stiles before finally emerging into an open pasture.

Go through the field and on reaching the stile turn sharply right, almost back in the direction from where you have just come. This steep path leads to a gate. Go through the gate and keep going straight ahead alongside the fence. Soon another stile is reached; cross it and continue towards the farmhouse at Peterel Field, this time with the wall on your left. Once the stile next to the farmhouse is reached continue straight ahead on the ensuing access track.

This track is now followed until it bends sharply to the right where a stile directly in front of you is crossed. Proceed up the field to reach a gate in the fence. To the left can be seen the racecourse mentioned in the previous section. As the crest is finally and somewhat thankfully reached another stile is crossed and the path starts to head diagonally right across the field towards the farm house at Plover Hill.

As the farm is passed a stile is seen directly ahead. Cross this to arrive at the road. Ignoring the routes both right and left proceed straight ahead where the road begins the long descent into Hexham. As the descent becomes more severe the road eventually culminates at a junction. Turn right and follow the road to the traffic lights. By bearing right the road leads into the heart of this superb Northumbrian town and a chance to visit one of the most historic Abbeys in this country.

FACILITIES IN HEXHAM

Hexham is the biggest town on this walk and as you would expect a vast array of facilities beckons. B&B's, pubs and shops are plentiful but tonight, for a pleasant change it is the hardy backpacker who will benefit most from their visit to this ancient market town. For it was here I discovered what I personally consider to be one of the premier camp sites (along with Sykeside) this country has to offer. In the course of my adventures I have stayed at countless sites throughout the United Kingdom but an overnight stay here was an absolute joy. Awarded the David Bellamy Conservation Gold Award and deservedly so, the camper can marvel at the attractive sight of Roe Deer, Red Squirrels, Rabbits and a host of other creatures as they wander aimlessly through the confines of the grounds in the knowledge they are not going to be disturbed by the mature clientele resident on site. (Children are not encouraged here as the welfare of the animals is paramount in the eyes of the owners.)

As soon as the site in the centre of this busy town is entered it soon becomes blatantly obvious that this family run business has been lovingly nourished over a number of years. Nothing, it appears, has escaped their meticulous attention. This is one campsite I can honestly say I will revisit many more times in the future.

As Hexham is the largest town we visit on this walk finding venues is more complicated than normal. I have therefore included the following two sections to aid you on your visit.

DIRECTIONS FOR BACKPACKERS

To get to the Riverside Leisure site proceed through the town to reach the Abbey. From the market place opposite walk downhill, along Gilesgate. At the bottom of the hill is a pub called the Skinners Arms. Continue straight ahead to meet the main road. Cross and then turn along the road next to interestingly named car dealers: 'Hexham Horseless Carriages'. This leads along a road which passes the bus depot to arrive at the playing fields. Turn left and the camp site is approximately 100 yards on the left.

PUB GUIDE

Pubs abound in Hexham and choice of venue a personal preference. However, as a guide for quality I can heartily recommend the Heart of England on Gilesgate where a wholesome and reasonably priced meal was attained, but for the Real Ale buff the Tap & Stile on Battle Hill is a must.

HEXHAM

Straddling the banks of the famous River Tyne lies the town of Hexham. This small market town was founded as early as the 7th century when St. Wilfred laid the foundations for the Benedictine Abbey.

Throughout the passage of time the town has been witness to a turbulent history. It was a battle near here that led to the end of the War of the Roses and the death of Henry VI. The battle was fought at Linnels Bridge which is approximately two miles south of the town. The Yorkists had been camped in Dipton Wood from where they began their charge, catching the Lancastrians in a ravine. With a steep bank to their rear they had no means of escape and consequently suffered heavy losses. The Duke of Somerset, who was leading the King's troops, was captured and taken to Hexham where he was subsequently tried and executed. Henry VI did manage to escape from Linnels Bridge but was soon caught and likewise executed.

Northumbria is the most northerly of all English counties and therefore suffered more than most from forages with the Vikings through to the marauding Scots. Construction of the magnificent Abbey began in AD 671 and was so nearly lost forever two hundred years later when it was burned to the ground by Halfdene the Dane and his Viking forces as they swept through the area. Only when the Archbishop of York gave the land to the Augustine monks in AD 1113 was the Abbey rebuilt, largely as you see it today.

A stroll around Hexham is a living history lesson. Any town which boasts a Tourist Information Centre in a 14th century gaol provides testament to its rich historical background. The Border History Museum is also contained within this impressive building and is essential viewing for all on this walk for it is now that the route enters 'Border Reiver' country and an understanding of this period will enhance your enjoyment.

'Reiver' was another term for the cattle thief and this sort of theft was certainly prevalent with the Anglo-Scottish border continuously being shifted and, with little in the way of law enforcement, the 'reivers' made a lucrative living.

So bad was the situation that many local farmers agreed to pay them a ransom to be left in peace. This would be in the form of black cattle or 'mails' as they were known, hence the origin of the word 'blackmail'.

The gaol was constructed in 1330 in stone which was liberated from the Roman camps which littered the surrounding countryside. The first ever specially built gaol in England, its thick stone walls hold a history that we may never fully realise. It continued to serve its purpose until as late as 1824.

Opposite the Abbey and still dominating the market place is the old gatehouse tower. Built in 1400 it was designed as a stronghold to withstand the too frequent attacks by the Scots.

As you pass under the archway the market place beckons, scene of one of the bloodiest battles ever seen in Hexham, for it was here in 1761 that the Hexham Riots took place. Angry crowds of miners from nearby Allendale were incensed at the prospect of being conscripted into the local militia and had gathered to vent their feelings. Troops from the North Yorkshire Militia took no chances and opened fire on the hordes. More than fifty people were killed and three hundred injured. From that day on the regiment became known as the 'Hexham Butchers'.

Since that fateful day the town has stood in relative calm and today attracts thousands of visitors from all over the world. Close to the remains of the Roman Wall and the accompanying forts, Hexham provides a good base for a holiday touring these historic sites.

The Tourist Information Office provides a plentiful supply of good quality literature on the area and it is plain to see that everyone concerned with promoting Hexham is rightfully proud of what is one of the highlights of this walk.

Whenever a multi-day walk is laid down towns are normally avoided at all costs and that is very understandable. However, in the case of Hexham, I make no apologies for taking the Lake to Lake right through the heart of a busy town. For any walker who has the time, a day exploring the delights of this place will be a day well spent and enjoyed.

HEXHAM ABBEY

Standing majestically in the heart of Hexham, the Abbey Church of St. Andrew dominates this small market town on the southern bank of the river Tyne. The birth of Hexham Abbey, as it is more commonly known locally, can be attributed to St. Wilfrid. Born shortly after Christianity was first brought to Northumbria, Wilfrid travelled to Rome and was inspired by the magnificent places of worship he encountered. On his return he was granted land by Queen Etheldreda of Northumbria and so started to recreate a monastery and church based on what he had encountered on his travels. Dedicated to St. Andrew this Benedictine monastery stood for one hundred and fifty years before decay led to a mass exodus by the local monks. Many years later as Norman rule swept England the fate of the monastery was restored. With their occupancy of this country they brought with them new ideas and put back the enthusiasm into the church.

In AD 1113 the Archbishop of York despatched Augustinian Canons to Hexham (or Hextildesham, as it was then known) to revive the church as a priory. Much of what can be seen today is the result of that task. The canons both lived and worked around the magnificent structure they created. For almost four hundred years the priory stood in relative calm until, in 1536, the canons took up arms to defend their church from the commissioners ordered in by Henry VIII as he seized control of all churches. Alas, after six months the canons were left with no alternative other than surrender and were abruptly evicted.

Since that time the Abbey has served the local community as its Parish Church. Taking time to explore this superb Abbey is well worthwhile and a number of publications which provide a full history of the interior are available to enhance your visit. On my visit I purchased an explanatory leaflet (50p) from the Tourist Information Centre just off the market place which I found invaluable as I explored the nooks and crannies of this splendid little Abbey.

With the passage of time parts of Hexham Abbey have had to be restored. In the middle of the 19th century the east end collapsed and was rebuilt by the famous Newcastle architect, John Dobson.

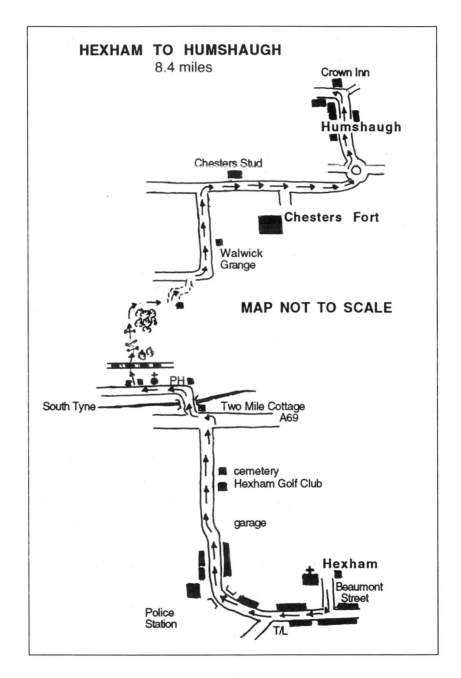

HEXHAM TO HUMSHAUGH
8.4 miles

Crown Inn

Humshaugh

Chesters Stud

Chesters Fort

Walwick
Grange

MAP NOT TO SCALE

PH

South Tyne

Two Mile Cottage
A69

cemetery
Hexham Golf Club

garage

Hexham

Beaumont
Street

Police
Station

T/L

HEXHAM TO HUMSHAUGH

8.4 miles / 13.5 Km

The following section involves a large amount of roadside walking.

To leave Hexham walk along Beaumont Street which leads past the Abbey and the Park and arrives at a junction where a memorial to Lieutenant Colonel George Elliott Benson, an officer killed in the Boer War, stands at the junction. At this point turn right and follow the road to eventually reach the traffic lights where Hexham was first entered. Continue straight ahead, this leads over a small bridge and past the Police Station. Continue to follow the road and as the built up area is finally vacated, the route passes Broadway Garage and, still following the road (keep to the right hand side), the route eventually passes Hexham Golf Club and the cemetery before finally culminating at the junction with the A69. Take great care in crossing this extremely busy thoroughfare.

Once over the dual carriageway turn left and proceed to a junction only twenty yards away on the right, where Two Mile Cottage is found on the junction. At this point turn right and follow the quiet back road as it winds its way downhill. Cross the bridge which spans the River South Tyne. Directly ahead is the Boatside Inn. Turn left and follow the road passing the Methodist Church. On reaching the next house a sign 'Public Bridleway - Fourstones' is found on the right. Turn up this lane and cross the railway line at the stiles.

As the houses are passed the path leads straight ahead through the trees to a gate. Once through begin the steady climb up the field keeping the fence to your left. This arrives at another gate, at which turn left but ignoring the first gate take the gate directly in front. The enclosed path leads gently to the right and begins to climb once again. Keeping the fence on your right a gate is passed through. Proceed along this well trodden path and through another gate whereupon the fence should now be to the left. This leads over a short brow where yet another gate is found in the corner of the wood.

This well defined track now leads all the way through the woods and eventually reaches, you guessed it, a gate. Continue straight ahead and as a cottage is approached bear left towards the gate. Go through the gate and you are now on the access track. Follow this all the way as it starts to sweep right and then left to arrive at the road. Turn right and once again, unfortunate as it may be, we are condemned to road walking.

The route now passes Walwick Grange Farm and continues up to a junction with the B6318. Turn right and again follow the road past the Chesters Stud and then the entrance to Chesters Roman Fort. This road leads directly to a roundabout where the second exit, signposted 'Humshaugh' is taken. Proceed along this access road all the way until arriving in the centre of this small village.

FACILITIES ON THIS SECTION

After leaving Hexham facilities are strictly limited. After a couple of miles there is the Boatside Inn but little else presents itself before arrival in Humshaugh, where a pub and a couple of shops serve the sparse population.

The Crown Inn, Humshaugh

CHESTERS FORT and the ROMAN OCCUPATION OF BRITAIN

After the brief foray of Julius Caesar into Britain in 55 and 54BC Rome had enjoyed a fairly peaceful existence with this country. Trade and diplomatic links seemed to work well but after the expulsion of a prominent Roman sympathiser in AD 43 it provided the opportunity not only for Rome to extend its vast empire but also for the Emperor to prove his worth.

Claudius had succeeded the imperial throne in the wake of such illustrious leaders as Augustus and Tiberius and many Romans regarded him as unworthy to follow such legends. Now with this diplomatic dispute the chance was quickly seized to suppress the doubters. England was invaded and the progress of the well machined force was swift. Roman rule overcame most of southern England. The occupying force consolidated its position and, with the exception of Boudicca's revolt in AD 60 relative calm prevailed.

By the early 70s the Romans started to turn their attentions more and more to the north. Heavily fortified strongholds were built at both York and Chester, providing platforms from which the occupation could be extended. When Agricola was appointed governor in AD 78 the Brigantes in the north had already felt the might of the Roman Army and a full network of forts now controlled the whole of England.

Seven years later, after a series of military campaigns, Agricola's forces had secured much of southern Scotland but as they advanced further and further north they met with more stubborn resistance. With men and resources severely stretched the Romans withdrew from Scotland. By the turn of the century little evidence of Roman influence could be found north of the border. In AD 117 Hadrian became Emperor, political upheaval in Rome raged and the niggling insurgence by the Scots into the furthest outpost of the empire constantly ensured the attention of the new regime, so much so that in AD 122 Hadrian became the first Emperor to visit Britain since Claudius, all those years previous.

In order to stop the skirmishes along the frontier Hadrian ordered the building of a wall, a wall which would stand more than fifteen feet high and stretch 76 miles from the bridge at Newcastle to Bowness on the Solway Firth. Work began immediately and was carried out by Roman Legionary troops (in the latter stages of construction auxiliaries, non-Roman troops were used). Before any barrier was erected the smaller forts (milecastles) were built, with two smaller turrets between each of the milecastles. These fortifications would serve as home to thousands of troops. By AD 130 one of the greatest engineering feats of the day was nearing completion. Apart from the obvious objective, to deter unwanted visitors, the wall also marks the end of expansion; the mighty Roman Empire would diminish from here onwards.

CHESTERS FORT

It is generally agreed in historic circles that the original name for the fort was 'Cilurnum'. Possibly derived from the Celtic, this means 'cauldron', a possible reference to the nearby swirl pool in the Tyne, but this is pure hypothesis. After its construction the fort housed a vast and varied number of military personnel. By its position on level ground and by the position of the gates it can be safely assumed that the fort originally housed cavalry units. In fact it is known that the 'Augusta Cavalry', named for their valour, were some of the earliest inhabitants. By the middle of the second century it is known that infantry garrisons were occupying the fort. A discharge paper dated AD 146 was discovered here showing the presence of Roman Auxiliaries. (Auxiliaries were seconded from all parts of the empire. If they survived their service they were awarded Roman citizenship upon their retirement, and all of the benefits associated with such an honour.) Other garrisons which occupied Chesters include the First Cohort of Dalmatians from present day Yugoslavia, the First Cohort of Vangiones from Germany and the Asturian Cavalry. Most of the splendid history we can now identify with Chesters remained buried for many centuries but we have a man called John Clayton to thank for its restoration, for it was he who excavated much of what you can see today when he inherited the land in 1832.

The layout of Chesters Roman Fort

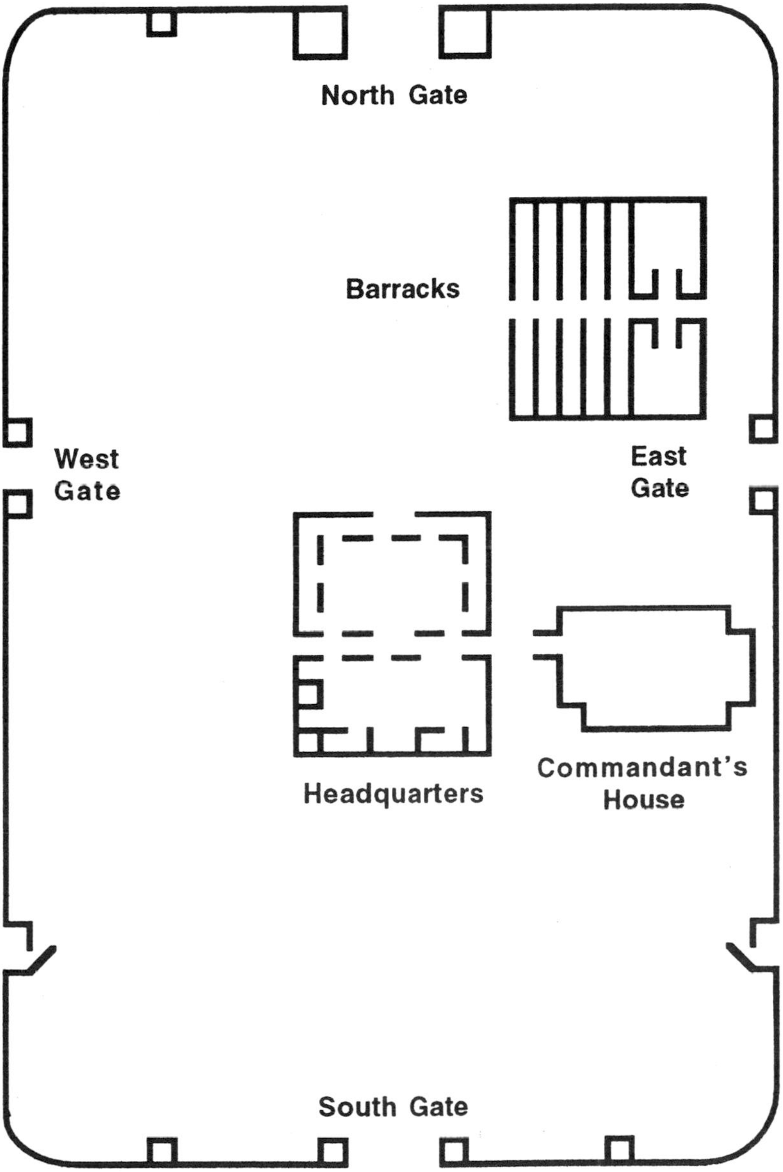

North Gate

Barracks

West
Gate

East
Gate

Headquarters

Commandant's
House

South Gate

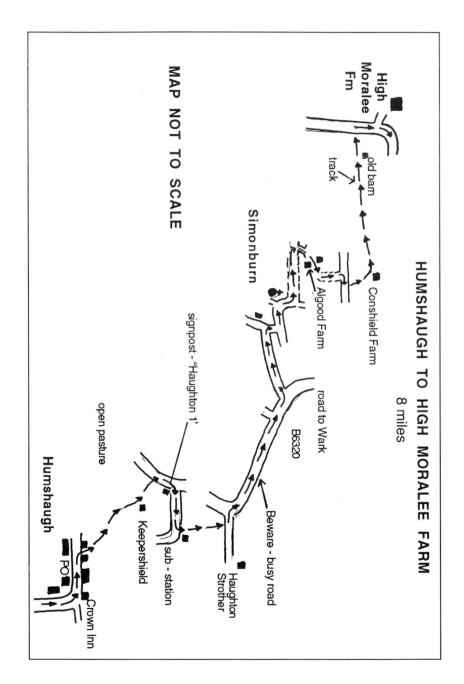

MAP NOT TO SCALE

HUMSHAUGH TO HIGH MORALEE FARM

8 miles

High Moralee Fm

old barn

track

Simonburn

Conshield Farm

Algood Farm

road to Wark

B6320

signpost - "Haughton 1'

open pasture

Beware - busy road

Humshaugh

PO

Crown Inn

Keepershield

sub - station

Haughton Strother

HUMSHAUGH TO HIGH MORALEE

8.0 miles / 12.9 Km

On reaching the centre of the village follow the road around to the left opposite the Crown Inn. Walk along the right hand side of the road, pass the Post Office and telephone box and soon a signpost saying 'Keepershield' is found on the right. Soon the track recedes into a path. Cross the footbridge, go through the gate and bear left up the side of the field.

After passing through a gap in the next hedge a stile is finally reached. Cross and aim for the next stile which can be seen ahead. Look directly ahead where a lone cottage stands; head straight across the field aiming for this building. On arrival go through the gate to the left and start to bear left across the pasture on the well defined path. Once through the stone gate way a track then leads back to the road. Turn right and follow the road for only a short way, past the farm house to a junction on the right signposted 'Haughton 1'.

Proceed down this quiet country lane until the road turns sharply to the right; at this point vacate the road and turn left along the path, past the electricity sub-station. The path follows along the side of the wall, through a couple of gates. and finally ends as an access track is met. Turn left and then right onto the road. There now follows a hazardous but unavoidable road walk. Keep walking along the road, pass the junction on the left for 'Fourstones' and keep to this road until the next turning on the left appears.

At last the busy road is vacated and a quiet track leads to a junction at the top of the lane. Turn right. The track now drops sharply and at the bottom turn left. This leads uphill to the tiny hamlet of Simonburn. As the village square is reached follow to the right and just before arriving at the shop turn left up the access road. Soon the road becomes a track and drops into the wood where a bridge is crossed. Once over continue straight ahead up the hill.

At the top as the copse finishes a gate is passed through. Continue straight ahead until a farm is seen on the right. The route now drops and crosses the burn at the bridge. Go through the gate and proceed up to the farm. Pass between the farm buildings onto the access track ahead. Follow this track all the way to meet the road. Turn right and after approximately 100 yards turn left through a gate (next to the overtaking space). Keeping to the side of the hedgerow climb the hill and through another gate.

At this point start to head diagonally left which will bring you to the entrance of a farm. Without entering the farm turn left and follow the track along the side of the wall. A pleasant stroll now ensues. A gate is passed through and then, as an empty barn is spotted on the right and the wall turns at right angles away from you, continue straight ahead. With care a green trail can be seen and followed. By maintaining this direction a road is soon reached. Turn right, and ignoring the stile on your left continue down the road passing High Moralee Farm on the left.

FACILITIES ON THIS SECTION

Once out of the pleasant village of Humshaugh there are no facilities available along this section of the route.

HANDY HINTS

Navigation is a key element of any expedition; your compass is vital to way finding and you should be proficient with it. But what happens if you lose it or break it? As long as you can find North you are still capable of finding your route. This can be done by using an ordinary wrist watch.

Place a small stick in the ground so that it casts a shadow. Place your watch on the ground so that the hour hand points along the shadow. Find the point on the watch midway between the hour hand and 12 o'clock (1 o'clock during BST). A line from the centre of the face points due South. If you have a digital watch you will need to draw out the clock face with the correct time showing.

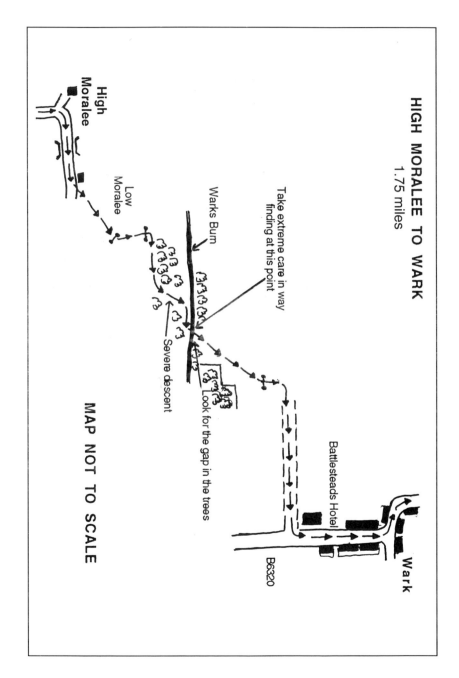

HIGH MORALEE TO WARK

1.75 miles

MAP NOT TO SCALE

High Moralee

Low Moralee

Warks Burn

Take extreme care in way finding at this point

Severe descent

Look for the gap in the trees

Battlesteads Hotel

B6320

Wark

HIGH MORALEE TO WARK

1.75 miles / 2.8 Km

On passing the entrance to the farm follow the road as it bends sharply to the right. At the bottom the road crosses the stream and begins the drag up the other side. Go through the gate and past Low Moralee Farm. Immediately after passing the farm a path on the left is discovered, signposted 'Public Footpath - Wark'. Go through the gate and walk diagonally right across the open field. This leads to another gate in the corner of the field. At this point turn sharply left and follow the line of the fence to a wooden gate, go through and turn right. Within twenty yards the path suddenly drops down to the left on what can only be described as a terrifying so-called path.

Descend with great care and at the bottom turn right alongside the stream. Walk downstream for approximately fifty yards and a gap in the trees on the far bank reveals the crossing point. Cross the stream and begin the climb up the field, keeping well away from the copse on the right. As the summit is reached a gate is passed through. The route now drops down the field with the fence to your right and swings right through another gate onto an access track.

Follow this track all the way to join the road. Turn left and, passing the Battlesteads Hotel, follow the road for the short journey into Wark.

FACILITIES ON THIS SECTION

There are no facilities available along this section of the route until you reach Wark.

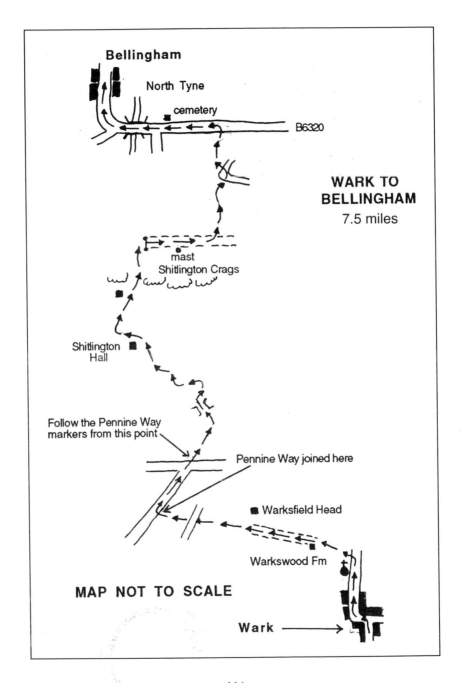

Bellingham

North Tyne

cemetery

B6320

**WARK TO
BELLINGHAM**
7.5 miles

mast
Shitlington Crags

Shitlington
Hall

Follow the Pennine Way
markers from this point

Pennine Way joined here

Warksfield Head

Warkswood Fm

MAP NOT TO SCALE

Wark ⟶

WARK TO BELLINGHAM

7.5 miles / 12 Km

In the centre of the village bear left, still following the road, and then right. The road is now followed all the way out of Wark and past St. Michael's church. Approximately 50 yards past the church turn left over the stile next to the signpost 'Warksfield Head'. Cross the metal footbridge and over the stile.

Keeping the fence to your right proceed up the hill, cross another stile and onto the track in front. The rise continues and as the track bears left at the summit the route goes straight on with the fence now on the left. Within 200 yards the path crosses back to the other side of the fence but still maintains the same direction. Cross another stile. At the top a gateway leads onto a track. Continue straight ahead to pass the cottages.

Proceed to the second gate; once through bear left (fence to your left), very soon to cross back once more (fence on your right). Although the directions sound confusing by remembering to follow a straight line you are on course. Continue up the track, through another gate until open fell is reached.

The route bears gently left to a stile in the corner of the field. Cross the road and over the other stile opposite (Pennine Way 0.5 miles). Continue straight ahead over the ensuing stiles, through a gate and to the road. Turn right and follow this quiet access road to the bottom of the hill. Directly ahead a stile is crossed; follow this well defined footpath known as the Pennine Way.

The route swings left and crosses the footbridge whereupon a right turn is made, over another bridge and alongside the stream to a gate on the left. Proceed through two gates before joining the track which bends to the right. As the farm is passed the route bears left and descends. After yet another gate the way bears right alongside the fence. After crossing the burn the route rises sharply once more to a stile in front of Shitlington Crags.

Continue the climb to the left of the mast to where a marker post is found at the summit. Way markers lead to a stile cross and turn left; onto the track. Pass the mast and continue until the Pennine Way marker is reached. Turn left and maintain a straight line to the top of the hill where a large signpost is found. Proceed straight down the field following the line of posts to the stile. Cross and turn left onto the track. After 100 yards a sign leads you over the stile and down the open moor. One more stile is crossed before arriving at the road.

Once onto the road turn left and follow this all the way until just prior to the bridge over the North Tyne a turning on the left is met. At this point the route actually turns left, but for those staying overnight in Bellingham the road is followed all the way into the village. If not turn left at this junction and refer to the next section.

FACILITIES ON THIS SECTION

The village of Wark provides a couple of good Pubs providing meals and sandwiches and the village shop is well stocked. With the exception of Wark there is little else before arrival in Bellingham.

BELLINGHAM

(pronounced Bellin-jum)

Situated at the foot of some of the most barren moorland this country has to offer the small town of Bellingham stands proudly on the banks of the North Tyne. With a population of approximately 1,200 the town is without doubt the most important in the area and, on this walk, is the last link with the public transport system. Do not rely on public transport after leaving Bellingham.

The history of the town can be traced back to mediaeval times. In fact it is recorded that at one time a castle stood here belonging to the King of Scotland's Forester, although no evidence remains. As with so many churches in the heartland of the famous saint Bellingham church is dedicated to the memory of St. Cuthbert.

Whilst the original building was demolished in the 12th century another church was erected and its massive stone roof makes it unique in England. Originally the roof had been constructed from timber but after raids from the marauding Scots (yes, them again) in which the church had been burnt down twice the new roof was laid and consisted of six-sided stone ribs being overlaid with stone slabs. It worked.

Dating as far back as the thirteenth century Bellingham boasted the largest wool fair in this country. A mill belonging to the De Bellingham family was situated within the town. Today, as then, Bellingham was the centre of trade within the Redewater area. As the town is entered on the Lake to Lake Walk, a field on the right, just after crossing the bridge: bears an inscribed nameplate 'The Irishmen's Graveyard'. This is not some romantic name from folklore but the actual burial site of approximately one hundred men who died during the construction of the Catcleugh Reservoir when cholera hit the area. After being buried here the field was not allowed to be used for any purpose for 100 years.

Other items of historical interest include the cannon which can be seen in the square. This is a 'Ginggall' and was captured from the Chinese by Admiral Sir Edward Charlton during the Boxer rebellion. The statue in the square is a memorial to the local men who lost their lives during the Boer War. Below the churchyard is St. Cuthbert's Well, known locally as 'Cuddy's Well'; the waters were reputed to hold mysterious healing powers and folklore would have us believe that one Sunday a young girl was found sewing on the Sabbath and her hand was paralysed. Water from the well was used to bathe the hand and she was miraculously and instantly cured. Folklore plays a big part in rural communities and the most famous of all Northumbrian Tales is the story of *"The Bellingham Longpack"*. Are you sitting comfortably (not if you've been walking for eleven days)?

Then I shall begin.

Our story begins in 1723 at Lee Hall. Lord of the manor Colonel Ridley was away in London and left the Hall under the care of a maid servant called Alice and two male servants.

One afternoon, in the depth of winter, a pedlar called at the Hall seeking a night's lodging. Although he was refused he was given permission to leave his heavy pack which would be picked up the following morning. The pedlar made his farewells and left.Uneasy about such a pack Alice could not resist making a more detailed inspection of it. Lighting a candle she moved closer when, to her absolute horror, it moved. Panic stricken, she screamed.

Coming to her assistance one of the male servants, old Richard, calmed the distraught girl and assured her that the pack was right enough. As they talked, a young cattle herder called Edward appeared. Hearing the story he proposed emptying the contents of his old military gun, for some reason called Copenhagen, into the pack.

This he proceeded to do and stood back in total shock as a roar and the final throes of death could be heard coming from the pack as blood gushed all over the stone floor. When the pack was opened the body of a man, who had been hidden inside, was discovered.

It was now obvious that the man had been part of a plot to rob the Hall and there was no doubt in Edward's mind that his co-conspirators would return during the night. After calling in a number of the Colonel's workers Edward sat back to await the robbers. At midnight (it always is) Edward blew the silver windcall found in the pack. Within minutes several horsemen arrived and entered the court gate.

As Edward fired Copenhagen into the faces of the intruders the other workers let fly with a simultaneous volley of shots. When the smoke cleared four men lay dead.

During the night the corpses were removed and no-one was ever brought to task to justify the slaughter.

In the churchyard can be seen the famous Long Pack Tombstone where, legend would have us believe, the pedlar was buried. Only one problem, the tombstone is almost certainly mediaeval.

FACILITIES IN BELLINGHAM

Bellingham offers a wide choice of facilities. Three pubs serve the village and an array of shops provide ample opportunity to stock up. The campsite is centrally situated (next to the Police Station) and there is a good Tourist Information Centre for inquisitive visitors.

The Boer War Memorial, Bellingham

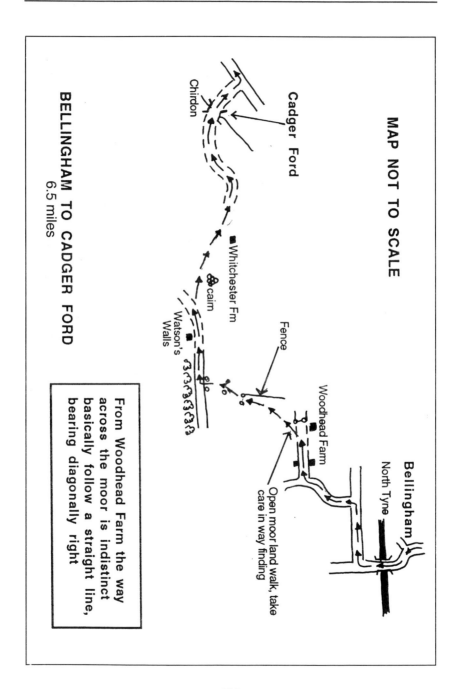

MAP NOT TO SCALE

Cadger Ford

Chirdon

■ Whitchester Fm

🐚 cairn

Watson's
Walls

Fence

Woodhead Farm

Bellingham

North Tyne

Open moor land walk, take
care in way finding

BELLINGHAM TO CADGER FORD
6.5 miles

From Woodhead Farm the way
across the moor is indistinct
basically follow a straight line,
bearing diagonally right

BELLINGHAM TO CADGER FORD

6.5 miles / 10.5 Km

And so, for many, we start the final day of this trek. If you have stayed overnight in Bellingham then you will need to retrace your steps back over the bridge and up to the first junction on your right. Turn right and follow the quiet tree lined back road until passing a farmhouse on the right. Go past and take the next turning on the left. This is an access track which leads up the moor.

There now follows a steady climb. As the track bends sharply to the right another track is found on the right, signposted 'Public Bridleway- Pundershaw 3'. The track leads past a cottage. As the last farm house, Woodhead Farm, is reached a stake post can be seen on the left. From this point way finding is difficult and time should be taken to ensure the correct route is being followed across the moor. Turn left at this point.

Although the trail is almost indistinguishable the route bears gently right. As the horizon is reached another marker post is found. Continue in a straight line across the open fell which leads to the side of a wall to a gate at the bottom. Go through the gate and walk straight ahead up the moor. No path can be seen but as the top is reached a fence can be seen to the right. Follow the line of the fence to arrive at another gate. Go through and bear right up the bridleway, which again is almost indistinguishable. Do not be fooled by a more evident trail which becomes apparent on the left.

Continue straight ahead and soon a gateway is reached in the corner of the pasture. From this gateway proceed directly ahead (stand between the posts of the gate and look directly ahead), where a very faint trail leads to the top of the moor. Ahead can be seen the line of the forest. Continue straight ahead to arrive at the gate. Turn right onto the track. Follow this track for the long drag to the cottage which can be seen at the top of the hill (Watson's Walls).

Continue straight past the cottage and bear right at the junction of tracks. Soon the track disintegrates but by maintaining a straight line a gate is soon reached. Go through and continue up the incline to the cairn at the top, where the views across Northumbria are exceptional. The route now bears gently right to a large signpost on the moor saying 'Cadger Ford'. Follow the bridleway in a straight line now dropping down the moor. To the right can be seen a farm and a gate, ensure you are well left of these.

After a couple of marker posts a railway sleeper bridge is crossed and a gate reached. Go through and follow alongside the fence which bears right to arrive at a track. Turn left onto the track and follow this all the way down off the moor. This leads through a gate and over the bridge at Cadger Ford to meet the road.

FACILITIES ON THIS SECTION

After leaving Bellingham we once again head into open countryside for the rest of the journey to Kielder. Not surprisingly there are no facilities whatsoever from this point on until the tiny hamlets of Stannersburn and Falstone are reached. Packed lunches are therefore the order of the day.

HANDY HINTS

Sometimes even the most obvious items we need to carry are overlooked. During my years of training others the one item I find people tend to forget when venturing onto an expedition are their sunglasses. Be it summer or winter sunglasses are vital; not only do they give protection during long summer days but they also prevent snow blindness, something which can easily happen, even in this country. They also provide good protection for the eyes in strong winds. Should you forget or lose your glasses what can you do as a temporary measure? Simple. Take a piece of card and cut two very narrow eye-slits, use a spare boot lace for a fastener and you will have the protection needed.

Remember - always protect the lips, eyelids and nostrils from the elements as these are the most sensitive parts at risk. Carrying a lip salve in the first aid kit is always a good idea.

Participants enjoying a day out with the DYES Scheme

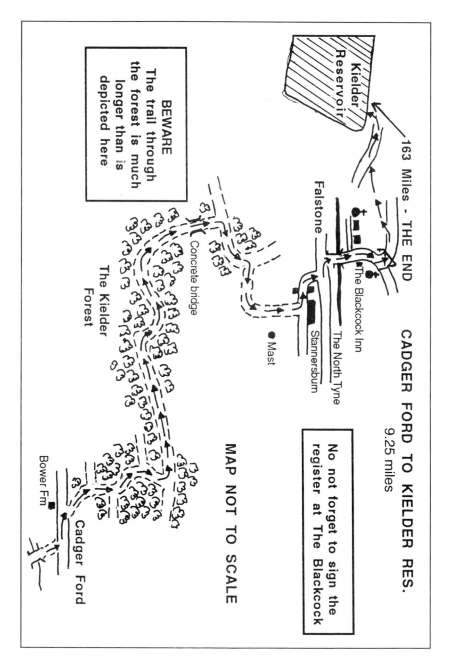

163 Miles - THE END

CADGER FORD TO KIELDER RES.

9.25 miles

No not forget to sign the register at The Blackcock

Kielder Reservoir

Falstone

The Blackcock Inn

The North Tyne

Stannersburn

Mast

Concrete bridge

The Kielder Forest

MAP NOT TO SCALE

Bower Fm

Cadger Ford

BEWARE
The trail through the forest is much longer than is depicted here

CADGER FORD TO KIELDER RESERVOIR

9.25 miles / 14.9 Km

On reaching the road turn left and proceed up the road for only a short distance where, just prior to the farm which can be seen on the left, a track is taken on the right. On the final section the walk now enters the mass of Kielder Forest. As tracks constantly change within the forest the route has to follow permanently set tracks.

You are now entering the Kielder Forest. Follow the track as it begins the climb. At the first summit the track bends left and then rises once more. Ignore a track which joins from the right and continue straight ahead. The route now starts to drop and a junction is reached. Take the track to the right; this in turn leads to another junction at which turn left.

Continue to follow what seems like a never ending track but eventually as the route drops once again a gate is reached. Go through and round to the right, over the concrete bridge. The track now bears left and begins to climb once more and comes to yet another junction, at which turn right. Once over the hill the route bends to the left and begins a descent.

At the bottom a junction is found on the right. Turn right at this point and follow the less distinct track. Once again it climbs and bends left to pass the mast before a steep descent leads to a gate and the tiny village of Stannersburn. Turn left and walk along the road, past the Pheasant Inn until it meets the main road. At this point turn left and proceed for a short distance before turning right and following that road across the bridge and into Falstone.

In the heart of the village can be found the Black Cock Inn (where the finishing register is kept); go straight past the pub and continue up the road and under the bridge. Once under turn left and follow the road until a track (the old railway line) is taken on the left. Go through the gate and follow this track all the way. As the line ends a track is joined and bears left. Pass the farmhouse on the left and continue up this road. As the climb finally reaches the top and a path on the left leads past the stone monuments you have finally arrived at the end of the walk, with a superb view across Kielder Water. There will be no fanfares and, as with any long distance walk, the only person with any sense of the importance of your arrival will be you.

YOU HAVE COMPLETED THE LAKE TO LAKE WALK
CONGRATULATIONS

All that is left to do is to retrace your steps back to the Black Cock Inn, sign the register and toast your success. Do not forget to leave your name and address as I will be proud to send you your certificate free of charge.

FALSTONE

This quiet and unassuming village at the eastern end of Kielder Water provides the finish for the Lake to Lake Walk. Within its confines you can secure superb accommodation at the Post Office, and then toast your success with a well earned pint or two at the Black Cock Inn.

The Black Cock Inn, Falstone

KIELDER RESERVOIR

Opened by Her Majesty Queen Elizabeth II in 1982 Kielder Water is the largest man made lake in Europe. It was originally built to serve the industrial conurbation of Newcastle but with the depression in heavy engineering the reservoir has since been used to supply other regions with their water in times of drought and has become a popular venue for visitors seeking water sport activities.

After the demands of the first World War Britain's timber supply was totally exhausted. Planting the more robust broad-leaved trees was not feasible as they take a hundred or more years to mature, and so the Kielder forest region grew rearing more than 120 million Scots Pine, Japanese Larch and Sitka Spruce, all of which are still grown, supplying the majority of the demand of this country as well as others.

Building the reservoir, as you can imagine, was a huge task. Work first started in 1975; however work on the dam itself did not commence for more than a year later. As the work load increased so did the workforce. At one point more than 750 men were working on this project. By 1982 a dam 1250 yards long, 170 feet high and 423 yards wide held back more than 44,000 million gallons of water, The lake is more than seven and a half miles long and covers nearly 2,700 acres.

Running under the dam is the huge access tunnel, used by the workers who maintain this huge engineering feat. Although not open to the public the tunnel is opened each year as hundreds of athletes from all over the country pass through on the annual 'Kielder Run'.

The village of Kielder is small to say the least and the lack of public transport made it impossible to finish the walk here, as was originally planned. However mention should be made of Kielder Castle. Now the Forestry Commission's Information Centre, it was originally built in 1775 for the Duke of Northumberland as a shooting lodge.

A WALK AROUND KIELDER WATER

Having already walked more than one hundred and sixty miles you will not take kindly to yours truly suggesting a walk around the lake.

However it is well worth considering as the wildlife alone makes it an interesting experience. If you would like to walk it (haven't you seen enough trees?) then return to where the walk finished and follow the markers for 'The Kielder Circuit' which starts in the car park. Be warned, the route follows tracks for most of the way and is not an easy route to accomplish.

Author working on his next book

A TIME TO REFLECT

The end of any long distance walk always seems to be a bit of an anti-climax. You have arrived at your destination and another great journey has finally ended. But as you sit and celebrate, why not take time to reflect on your achievement. You have just walked from the largest lake in England to the largest man made lake. Throughout that time there will have been moments of despair (especially the road walking) but now is the time to look back and remember the experience you have undergone.

It seems an age since the comfort of the Royal Oak in Bowness was vacated; the stroll along the shores of Windermere, High Sweden Bridge and that climb over Scandale Pass. Think back to the wonderful views across Ullswater, the stark contrast as the Eden Valley was passed through. Did you call at the Newby Hall Hotel? The bustling town of Appleby and then of course the rigours of the North Pennines, miles of bleak moorland and difficult way finding. The relief of arriving in Middleton in Teesdale and then up once more over Bollihope to Weardale. Who could ever forget the Allenheads Inn and the magnificent Abbey at Hexham. Then, arrival at Kielder and the fulfilment of another dream.

No doubt you have made many friends along the way, will have many special memories of your own and will return to some of the places visited in years to come. I hope you have enjoyed this walk and that it will encourage you to do more. For myself, I am off once again on my adventures and hope to be able to invite you to join me as I walk *In The Shadows of Saints & Soldiers*, the title of my next book, a walk I am developing which will cover the pilgrimages of the northern saints as well as touring the many battlefields in Northern England and Southern Scotland.

In the mean time . . . . good walking.